Gregor Mendel
and Heredity

ZUR
ERINNERUNG AN DIE ENTHÜLLUNG
DES
P. GREGOR MENDEL
DENKMALES
IN BRÜNN AM 2. OKTOBER 1910.

THEODOR CHARLEMONT WIEN

Pioneers of Science and Discovery

Gregor Mendel and Heredity

Wilma George

Fellow of Lady Margaret Hall and Lecturer in Zoology,
University of Oxford

PRIORY PRESS LIMITED

Other books in this series

Over page Memorial bronze of
Mendel, made for the unveiling of
the Mendel Monument in Brno in
1910.

SBN 85078 222 8
Copyright © 1975 by Wilma George
First published in 1975
Second Impression 1978
Priory Press Limited, 49 Lansdowne Place   Hove   Sussex   BN3 1HF

Text set in 12/14 pt. Photon Baskerville, printed by photolithography,
and bound in Great Britain at The Pitman Press, Bath

Contents

Illustrations

Guinie wheat, or
rather Indye wheat
fume do caule this Turci
wheat, but vniustlye.

Above American Indians sowing
their corn.

Left Indian corn, or maize, from P.
A. Matthioli *Commentarii Pedacii
Dioscoridis*, book 3, 1565.

Introduction

There is a five thousand year old Persian seal inscribed with horses' heads that shows a record of inheritance of mane and head shape through several generations. In England, Robert Bakewell (1725–1795) founded his famous herd of longhorn cattle by inbreeding: mating like with like. The American Indians improved their maize crop by outbreeding: crossing two unlike varieties of corn to get a variety with the qualities of both.

Sometimes these methods of selective breeding for inherited characteristics were successful. But

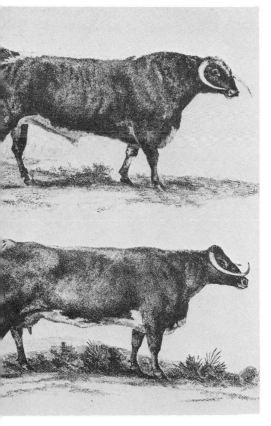

Below Robert Bakewell and his improved longhorn bull and cow.

sometimes the offspring would be more like one parent than the other, sometimes the offspring would be a mixture and, sometimes, the offspring would be a "throwback" to a grandparent. Thus, selective breeding worked in practice but the reasons for success or failure were not understood.

In 1865, Mendel showed in *Experiments in Plant Hybridization* how characteristics were inherited, how heredity depended on sexual reproduction, how the inheritance of likenesses followed simple mathematical rules. This is the basis of the modern science of genetics. By following Mendel's rules it is possible to understand how the size of corn cobs, the quality mane, the coat colour of cattle are inherited.

The rules have been found to apply to all plants and all animals. Thomas Aquinas (1225–1274) wrote that "idiots beget idiots." But inheritance in man is not so easy to study as it is in other animals.

Marriages cannot be arranged by the geneticist to study why there are albinos in one family, deaf mutes in another family and, in another family, blond hair and blue eyes. The geneticist must get his information from the results of marriages that have happened. But mathematical techniques have been invented for analysing this sort of information.

And advances in methods for identifying chemical differences between people have revolutionized the study of human inheritance. People have different chemical blood groups, different proteins, different colouring. Usually, these can be identified from only small samples of blood or skin. The way these chemical differences are inherited follows Mendel's laws.

Olive Green has a baby in hospital but, when the baby is brought to her, the label round the baby's wrist says Brown. Hazel Brown has a baby brought to her labelled Green. To find out which baby is which, a sample of blood is taken from both mothers and both babies.

Above Reverse side of a medal to commemorate the centenary of Mendel's papers to the Brno Natural History Society.

Olive's blood belongs to group O and so does the baby labelled Green. Hazel's blood is group O but baby Brown is group A. From these results, the question is not decided.

The fathers are asked to have their blood grouped. Herb Green, like his wife, is group O: it is impossible for their baby to be anything but group O. Ginger Brown is group A: in this case, he is the father of baby Brown. The labels were correct.

But group A Ginger Brown has also group O characteristics in his blood and so baby Brown could have been group O.

Could it have been predicted, therefore, that baby Green would be group O and baby Brown group A? Both Greens are group O and can have only group O children. Thus, according to the laws of inheritance, baby Green is predictable. But the prediction for baby Brown can be based only on probability. There was a 50% chance that baby Brown would be group A and the same chance that it would be O.

Predictability becomes important in the case of inherited diseases in a family. In most cases, the probability of the children inheriting a certain disease can be calculated: a 25% chance or a 50% chance. But it cannot be predicted that a particular child will or will not inherit it.

Mendel's biographer Hugo Iltis said that Mendel searched through the parish registers of Brno to find inherited characters in man. There is no evidence that he found what he was looking for. But the mathematical rules of chance that Mendel proved to be working in the inheritance of colour, shape and size in pea plants have been found to apply equally to man.

Gr. Piltsch
Mawrowitz
Jagnnitz
Bektar
Slatnik
Stabrowitz
Troppau
Zottig
Bretterdorf
Teschowitz
Schlak
Herlitz
Ekersdorf
Mladetzko
Hertitz
Teitersdorf
Schonstein
Witendorf
Langenberg
Rase
Petersdorf
Branek
Suche
Podoly
Bot
Neu Rode
Weivelsdorf
Carlsberg
Bronsdorf
Spachendorf
Dorf Deschen
Kuntzendorf
Statslowitz
Tilendorf
Lobnick
Raudenberg
Havdenpiltsch
Maywald
Lhota
Gratz
Arnsdorf
Christlorf
Medlitz
Niclowitz
Olbersdorf
Eichhorn
Waltersdorf
Neu Lublitz
Gersdorf
Morawitz
Meltsch
Dimatsau
Schönrowitz
Jaku
Kiwalko
tschhause
Dietersdorf
Herzogwald
Creutzberg
Ratkau
Wigstein
Hof
Prookersdorf
Grindersdorf
Alt Czechsd.
Dietersd.
Marksdorf
Paugersd.
Bautsch
N. Czechsd.
Notschinau
Oberdorf
Prise
Behrn
Indersdorf
Siebenhofen
Alte Lie
Schidwansdorf
Tschirin
Wiostadl
Imtsch
Oredsth
Neudorf
Schönwald
Altendorf
Unter dorf
Krodsth
Wunberg
Altegasse
Neudorf
Gr. Kloksd.
Kuntzendorf
Waltersd.
Domstadt
Reisend
Kl. Kloksdorf
Komin
Wolfsdorf
Gerlsdo
Petersdorf
Hertlsd
Kriegsdorf
Bernau
Gr.
Fune
Liebau
Trembsd.
Rudelzau
Sponau
Kl. Hermesdorf
Goperitzau
Sichertzau
Liebenthal
Laudmer
Joosdorf
Faschend
Swail
Olstatll
Linden
Lautsch
Laster
Groswass
Waltersdorf
Milbis
Schmidsau
Schertzen
Dobischwald
Polau
Zauchte
Weska
Eperswagen
Hermansd.
Gusdorf
Odrau
Pohorz
Habicht
Paskau
Heinrichswald
Wessull
Munkendorf
Hombock
Haslicht
Josehau
Biardlsd.
Irnsdorf
Hantzend.
Nierklowitz
Kozlan
Finfzuhüben
Punkendorf
Neudek
St. Petersdorf
ernitz
Przaslawitz
Duskabal
Rzika
NeuPrusinowitz
Mittelwald
Radelsdorf
Lhotky
Olspytz
Deut. Jasnik
Hurka
sedlitz
Doloplas
Ob. Augez
Schlakau
Ungersdorf
Bodhorz
Wrabuwky
Klogsdorf
Bolten
Blatendorf
Pohl
Witenber
chowitz
Waczenowitz
Wiklek
Kl. Hranik
Unt. Augezd
Stanimierwitz
Bohuslawka
Lautzka
Milenau
Sbawitsch
Welke
Wolfsdorf
Daub
Trschitz
Lypnan
Swerzow
Tupetz
Trnawka
Prahotisch
Weiskirchen
Kuntzend
Herniz
Katzendor
Suchonitz
Nedschowitz
Kl. Penschitz
Gr. Wisschitzko
Chiletz
Leipnick
Neugestift
Speitsch
Teplice Hews
Tanowit
Wyssok
Baltzo
Kokor
Zabeczmlotha
Kl. Lhota
Radiwanitz
Beczwa
Helfenstein
Walschowitz
Czernotin
Skalitzka
Litschd
Milotitz
Justopetz
Wisoka
Leschno
Czekin
Winarz
Poppowitz
Butz
Ossek
Hlinsko
Kladnik
Oprostawir
Parschowitz
Jausty
Nemlitz
Prdlut
kawa
etnitz
Prösnitz
Ratzlawitz
Radotin
Oppatowitz
Trieschitz
Rauschky
Welts
Chori
Kl. Hadruby
Lhotka
P R E R A U E

1 *Johann takes the name of Gregor*

Among the rolling hills of mid-Czechoslovakia is a small village called Hynčice. In the nineteenth century it was called by the German name of Heinzendorf. In 1871, it had seventy-one houses with tiled roofs. The people who lived in the village were farmers and lime burners. One of the farmers was called Anton Mendel whose ancestors had been in the village since 1684.

As a young man, Anton had been in the army. When he came back to Hynčice, he took over a plot numbered 58 in the village and built a house with a tiled roof. He farmed his thirty "yoke" (about forty acres) of sloping meadow: ploughing, cultivating and trying to improve his stock of farm animals.

Anton was interested in fruit growing. He planted with fruit trees the field that sloped down from his house to the road. There Anton experimented with grafting new varieties of fruit, exchanging grafts and stock as well as advice with the priest in nearby Vražné (Gross-Petersdorf).

Left Map of the area where Mendel spent his early life, from C. Müller, 1802. Mendel's village, Hynčice, appears in the lower right hand corner as "Hantzend." just south of Odrau.

Below Sketch map of Czechoslovakia.

At the village school the principles of fruit growing were taught. It was unusual for a small village to have a school in those days. It was even more unusual to have one where the scientific principles of agriculture were taught.

In 1818, Anton married Rosine, the daughter of a gardener in the village. In July 1822 Johann was born, the second child and only son.

Johann went to the village school. The school-master, realizing that Johann was much cleverer than the other boys, persuaded Anton and Rosine to send him to a bigger school. So when Johann was eleven, he went to the Piarist College in Lipnik, an upper elementary school, about twenty kilometres from Hynčice. Again, he stood out from the rest so that, after a year in Lipnik, he was recommended for the Imperial Royal Gymnasium in Opava (Trappau), a high school about fifty kilometres to the north of Hynčice.

The farmer needed his son to work on the farm but, instead, he agreed to let him be educated. Anton was not rich and could not afford the full fees for the high school so Johann was entered on half rations. But whenever the carrier came to Opava he brought

Above The village school at Hynčice from a battered old photograph.

The school at Lipnik.

Johann a supply of fresh food from the farm. In this way, Johann managed to work through the first four "grammatical" classes at Opava.

Johann's school work was excellent. He was always graded first class with distinction and he qualified for the "humanities" classes of the upper school.

By this time, Anton was unable to pay for his son's education. He had been injured by a rolling tree trunk and was never again able to work his farm profitably. From the age of sixteen, Johann had to fend for himself. He became a qualified private tutor and, by giving private tuition and at the same time going to school, kept himself "after a fashion." But the hard mental work and inadequate food made him ill and, in the spring of 1839, Johann went home to the farm to work in the fields.

Back in Opava after a few months, he finished his studies and, in 1840, left the high school with a certificate of excellence.

Johann, at eighteen, now wanted to study philosophy at the University Philosophical Institute of Olomouc (Olmütz). He intended to pay for this by earning money from private tuition again. But "all his efforts remained unsuccessful," he wrote of himself later, "because of lack of friends and recommendations." This disappointment made him ill again and, this time, he spent a year at home on the farm to recover.

By 1841, Anton had to give up his farm. He sold it to Alois Sturm, the husband of his elder daughter Veronica. In making over the farm, Anton also made provision for Johann and for his younger daughter Theresia. Johann's share included a small sum of money if he "should enter the priesthood, or should in any other way begin to earn an independent livelihood." Theresia gave her share of the property to Johann and, with this and the private tutoring he finally obtained, he was able to study philosophy at Olomouc.

Above The house at Olomouc where Mendel lived when he was at the Philosophical Institute.

Above Brno in 1768.

"By a mighty effort," Johann wrote of himself, "he succeeded in completing two years of philosophy." But Johann was exhausted and "realized that it was impossible for him to endure such exertions any further." He could no longer put up with the insecurity of making his own way. "Therefore, after having finished his philosophical studies, he felt himself compelled to step into a station of life which would free him from the bitter struggle for existence." Johann followed the recommendation his father had made in 1841 and decided to enter the priesthood. "His circumstances decided his vocational choice."

Above The church of the Augustinian monastery at Brno

On 14th July, 1843, the Professor of Physics at Olomouc University, Friedrich Franz, wrote to a colleague at Brno (Brünn), the capital city of Moravia. He was answering an inquiry about suitable candidates for the priesthood. He wrote that he could recommend only one. "This is Johann Mendel, born at Heinzendorf in Silesia. During the two year course in philosophy he has had, almost invariably, the most unexceptionable reports and is a young man of very solid character."

On 9th October, 1843, Johann was admitted as a novice to the Augustinian monastery of Saint Thomas in Brno and took the name of Gregor.

2 The Monastery at Brno

The monastery at Brno was the intellectual centre of Moravia. The people spoke Czech but most of the monks were German. Mendel had little knowledge of Czech but was "willing," as Professor Franz wrote, "to devote himself to the mastery of the language during the years of theological study."

Most of the monks taught either at the University of Brno or at the High School. Visiting professors lodged at the monastery. The Abbot of the monastery Cyril Franz Napp (1782–1868) was Professor of Oriental Languages at the University. Aurelius Thaler (1796–1843) spent many years at the monastery while botanist at the Brno Philosophical Institute. He had made an important collection of the Moravian flora. He died in 1843 so Mendel just missed his chance to

Left Cyril Franz Napp, Abbot of the monastery in 1843.

Below The monastery.

study with him. But Thaler's collection of living plants in the monastery's botanic garden and the dried plants in the monastery's herbarium were at Mendel's disposal.

Mendel described himself studying these plants and the monastery's collection of local geological specimens: "His special liking for this field of natural science deepened the more he had the opportunity to become familiar with it."

Meanwhile his formal studies continued. In his first year, he attended, "with much liking and devotion," classes on church history, archaeology and Hebrew. The problems of existence seemed solved and he "regained his courage and strength."

In his second year at the monastery (when he was studying Greek, the Scriptures and Church Law) Mendel took the vows of obedience, chastity and poverty, in accordance with the rule of Saint Augustine. The following year, he was able to extend his studies towards his own interests. As well as studying the Church's teachings, Mendel went to courses in agriculture (apple and grape growing in particular) at the Philosophical Institute at Brno.

Left Refectory of the monastery.

Right Certificate of Mendel's studies in agriculture at Brno 1846.

Franz Diebl (1770–1859), who gave the lectures, was interested in the improvement of plants by hybridization.

In his fourth and final year of instruction, Mendel studied the practical aspects of being a priest such as teaching the catechism and preaching. He also learned Arabic, Syriac and Chaldaic (the languages of Arabia, ancient Syria and ancient Babylon). He was now twenty-five years old.

The following year, 1847, having been ordained sub-deacon, Mendel was made parish priest of the collegiate church. But Mendel had problems as a parish priest. He was too sensitive, too nervous. He suffered at school and became ill. As parish priest he suffered for the sufferings of others and found it unbearable to attend the dying. His problems were not made easier having to preach in Czech when his native language was German.

The Abbot appreciated Mendel's intellectual abilities and sympathized with his problems as parish priest. He gave him permission to work for the degree of Doctor of Philosophy. The Abbot then had Mendel appointed supply teacher to the Imperial Royal High School in Znojmo (Znaim). German, not Czech, was the language of this wine-growing district near Vienna.

On 9th October, 1849, Mendel took up his duties as supply teacher. He taught Greek and elementary mathematics for twenty hours a week. Mendel's experience of private tutoring during his school days helped him to understand his pupils and he was a great success.

The school described his "vivid and lucid method of teaching" and offered to make him a permanent member of the staff. But he would have to pass the teachers' qualifying examination which was usually taken after a course of training at university. He had not had this training but, nevertheless, he was persuaded to try the examination in the summer of 1850. He asked to be examined in natural history and physics.

The examination was held by the University of Vienna and was in three parts. For the first part, candidates were given eight weeks to write two essays. This was a preliminary test and only if they satisfied the examiners in the essays were candidates called to Vienna for the second and third parts of the examination. The two essay subjects that Mendel received were, for physics, on the chemical and physical properties of air and, for natural history, on volcanic and sedimentary rocks.

Mendel wrote his essays and the examiner in physics, Professor Baron von Baumgartner (1793–1865), reported that Mendel "writes simply, plainly and clearly, his method of exposition being orderly

Above Part of Mendel's answer to the biological question set by Rudolf Kner.

Left Mendel in 1848.

Above The secondary school at Znojmo.

and lucid. If the other examiners are as well satisfied as I am, the candidate should have a very favourable testimonial." But the Professor of Zoology, Rudolf Kner (1810–1869), was not satisfied.

Kner was influenced by the ideas of the great French paleontologist Georges Cuvier (1769–1832). The Frenchman regarded earth events as a series of independent creations, each brought to an end by some catastrophe of flood or fire or earthquake. There was no continuity. Kner was unlikely to be impressed by a statement from a student who wrote that "the creative energy of the earth remains active. So long as its fires still burn and its atmosphere still moves, the history of its creation is not finished." But, in spite of Professor Kner, Mendel was called to Vienna for the second part of the examination.

When Mendel arrived in Vienna, he found the examiners had changed their minds. It seems they had written to him to wait a year. However, since he was there, they allowed him to continue though, by then, Mendel was nervous.

Mendel again satisfied Professor Baumgartner with an essay on magnetism. For Professor Kner, he was asked to write an essay on the classification of mammals. Kner had already published a work on this subject but, in his essay, Mendel ignored the work of his examiner. He may never have heard of it. Mendel answered Kner's question according to what he remembered of a standard German work. He remembered the outline but was poor on detail and showed no interest in the theoretical aspects of classification. Mendel's "orderly and lucid" approach was not evident in this essay.

Mendel was called to the oral examination but failed.

Professor Baumgartner had been impressed by Mendel's work and advised the Abbot to send Mendel to the university at Vienna where he would be able to try the qualifying examination again.

3 *Vienna University*

For four terms, 1851–1853, Mendel was a student in the philosophical faculty in Vienna. World famous men were lecturing in the sciences in Vienna at this time and Mendel attended their courses in mathematics, physics and biology.

For experimental physics, he went to the lectures of Christian Doppler (1803–1853). In 1845, Doppler had shown how the pitch of a sound can seem to vary when it is moving in relation to the listener: the Doppler effect. For example, when a whistling train approaches very fast the note of its whistle seems to change. Doppler had been at Vienna University since 1850 and, in 1851 when Mendel attended his lectures, he was forty-eight and an acknowledged master. Although Doppler was interested mainly in the properties of sound and light waves, he was also interested in theoretical mathematics and geometry and lectured on these subjects.

Andreas von Ettingshausen (1796–1878) lectured on mathematical physics. He worked on problems in wave mechanics and, like Doppler, was interested in applying mathematics to physics. He was also an experimentalist and lectured on the use of apparatus and the design of experiments.

Mendel, with his distinct ability in physics, was greatly influenced by the mathematical approach to physics of these two men and influenced, too, by the methods of physical experiment. He acted as demonstrator in physics for a time and became familiar with the experimental method: to test an idea by a planned experiment.

Mendel attended Kner's zoology course. He went to lectures in paleontology, systematic botany and plant physiology. The plant physiology lectures, given by Unger, made the most impression.

Right Franz Unger.

Right Cellular tissue and isolated cells from several different plants (Matthias Schleiden, 1838).

24

Franz Unger (1800–1870) was a revolutionary in the biological sciences. He did not believe in the permanence of species but believed that the plant world had "gradually developed itself step by step." For this statement in *Botanical Letters* (1852), Unger was attacked by the Church and threatened with dismissal from the University.

Unger was a supporter of the cell theory. In 1838, Schleiden was looking for some underlying principle that would unify biology. Schleiden found it in the cell.

Matthias Schleiden (1804–1881) realized that all higher plants and animals were made up of cells which could be considered both as individuals and as united and dependent on one another in a whole plant or animal. These cells, making up whole plants and animals, he considered to be similar also to the single cells of the lower green plants, the algae. In 1842, Karl Wilhelm von Nägeli (1817–1891) had worked with Schleiden in Jena and had shown that cells divide and make more cells to give growth from the tips of plant shoots.

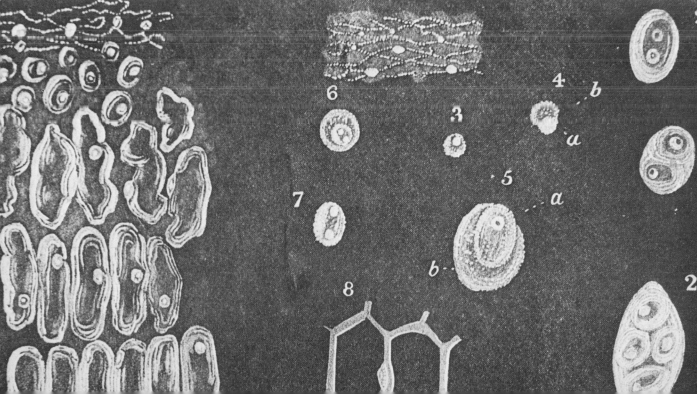

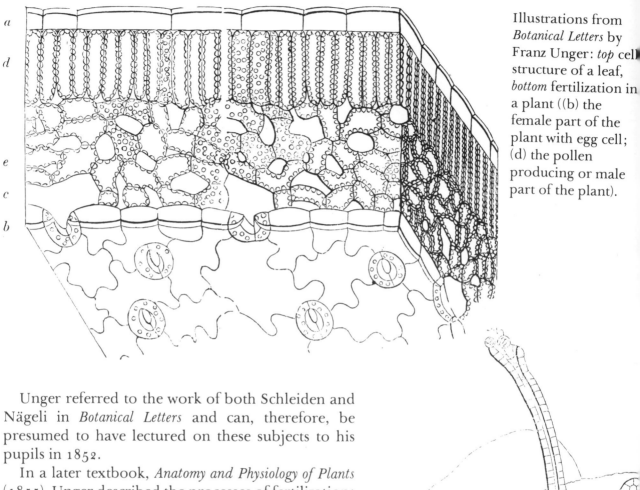

a

d

e

c

b

Illustrations from *Botanical Letters* by Franz Unger: *top* cell structure of a leaf, *bottom* fertilization in a plant ((b) the female part of the plant with egg cell; (d) the pollen producing or male part of the plant).

Unger referred to the work of both Schleiden and Nägeli in *Botanical Letters* and can, therefore, be presumed to have lectured on these subjects to his pupils in 1852.

In a later textbook, *Anatomy and Physiology of Plants* (1855), Unger described the processes of fertilization: the fusion of some element of maleness and some of femaleness. He wrote, too, about experiments in plant hybridization, the crossing of two unlike plants. He concluded that variations arose in natural populations and gave rise to new varieties and species.

So, during the four terms at Vienna University, Mendel learned that plants and animals are composed of cells. He learned of experiments in plant hybridization. And he learned the methods of experimentation in physics. This was one of the most influential periods of his life.

He returned to the monastery of Brno in July 1853.

The teaching staff of Brno Technical Modern School 1864. Mendel is sitting second from the right.

Above The pea-weevil *Bruchus pisi* from G. Cuvier *Le Règne Animal*, 1849.

The same year, he was appointed supply teacher to the new Technical Modern School in Brno. For the next fourteen years, he taught physics and natural history, always as a supply teacher. He could never qualify in the teachers' examination at Vienna. In 1856, he tried again but became too nervous even to finish the written part of the examination. But he was a gifted teacher, loved and respected by his pupils one of whom remembered years later the short fat monk with the twinkling grey eyes, dressed in a frock coat, trousers tucked into high boots and wearing a tall hat.

Before leaving Vienna, Mendel read a paper to the Zoological and Botanical Society on the moth *Botys margaritalis*, a pest of radishes. He had always been interested in crop improvement and the following year, 1854, he sent another paper on crop pests to the Society. This was a short description of the pea-weevil *Bruchus pisi*. Now he was elected a member of the Brno

Agricultural Society and could meet with local plant breeders and biologists from the university.

He started to make his own experiments in plant improvement on a small garden plot in the monastery. Soon he was crossing and selecting different varieties of peas and beans to improve their size and taste for the monastery table. By 1859, he had developed a variety of pea with bigger and sweeter seeds, fully fertile and easy to grow.

At meetings of the Natural Science Section of the Agricultural Society discussions were often on topics of more theoretical interest. Members argued about the problems of fertilization and reproduction in plants and animals, about growth and development. Franz Unger became a member of the Society in 1857.

Under the influence of Unger's work, Mendel had become interested in the cultivation of wild plants. Unger believed that species could change and he wondered how they could change. One possibility was that change could be brought about by hybridization: two species could be combined to give one new one. Another possibility was that change could be brought about by outside influences.

These outside influences could be, for plants, the nature of the soil in which they were growing, the amount of sunlight they received, the amount of rainfall. Some biologists, the most famous of whom was Jean-Baptiste de Lamarck (1744–1829), believed that these outside influences, that changed the form of the plant or animal, affected the whole organism, so that its changed form would be permanent and passed on to its offspring. In this way, species could be changed into new species by the direct effect of outside conditions.

Unger did not believe this. He had found from his own experiments that, although some species grew bigger or smaller according to the conditions of cultivation, others kept their characteristics in spite of being grown under new conditions.

Ranunculus Ficaria

Mendel repeated these experiments of Unger, bringing varieties of wild flowers into the monastery garden to grow under controlled conditions. He grew specimens of two lesser celandine species next to one another, in exactly the same conditions, for several seasons and found that they kept their separate characteristics. He must, therefore, have agreed with Unger who had written in *Botanical Letters*: "The endeavour to trace the diversities of species to the effects of outward influences, such as the nature of the soils, assuredly misses the true cause."

Mendel is said to have told a colleague at school that "nature makes little progress in the formation of species in this way: hence it must be something somewhat different."

Having reached this decision, Mendel looked for the "something somewhat different" in the outcome of hybridization experiments.

4 Plant Hybridization and Cell Theory before Mendel

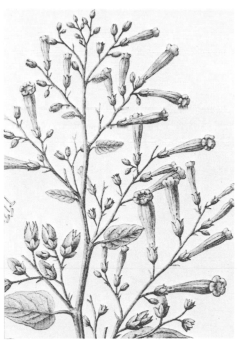

In the eighteenth century most men believed that species of animals and plants were fixed. New species were not created under natural conditions—still less could they be created by man. But the results of hybridizing plants gave puzzling results.

Carl Linnaeus (1707–1778), who for most of his life believed in the fixity of species, had seen two plant hybrids in the Botanic Gardens at Uppsala in Sweden. The unusual speedwell *Veronica* and the salsify-goat's beard plant *Tragopogon* were shown to be hybrids and to have some characteristics of both parents. Linnaeus believed these hybrids were new species and entered them in his *Species Plantarum* in 1753.

Experimental plant hybridization, however, started in 1760 when the German biologist Joseph Gottlieb Kölreuter grew his first hybrids in Leningrad (St. Petersburg).

In the introduction to his paper on plant hybridization, published in 1866, Mendel refers to the work of Kölreuter, Herbert, Lecoq, Gärtner and Wichura.

Kölreuter (1733–1806) knew that when two different plants were crossed they could give rise to hybrids. He did not believe that these hybrids would breed more like themselves and they were not, therefore, new species.

Kölreuter started his work with tobacco plants. He took pollen from specimens of *Nicotiana rustica* which has short flowers and a short style and put it on the styles of specimens of *Nicotiana paniculata* which has long flowers and a long style. From these crosses Kölreuter got seeds which grew into hybrid plants that were intermediate in character between the two parents. The plants were intermediate in the flower which was neither short nor long but medium in

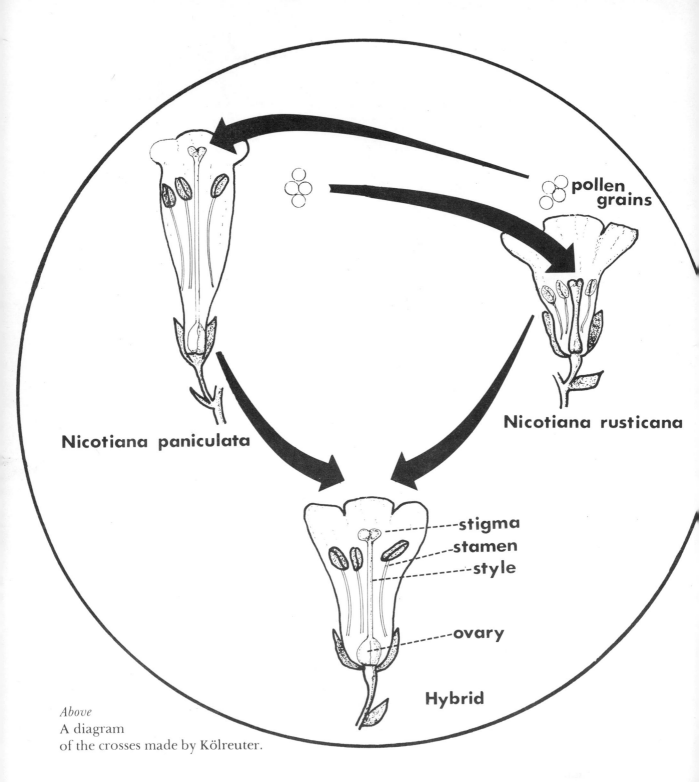

pollen grains

Nicotiana paniculata

Nicotiana rusticana

stigma
stamen
style

ovary

Hybrid

Above
A diagram
of the crosses made by Kölreuter.

length. The flower was neither red nor white in colour but pink. Both the branching of the plant and the position of the flowers were intermediate between the parents.

Kölreuter measured and recorded thirteen characteristics of which all except the form of the stamens were intermediate in the hybrid. But when Kölreuter's hybrid plants grew up not one of them was self-fertile. The flower heads dropped off and there were no seeds. To Kölreuter, this was "one of the most wonderful of all events that have ever occurred upon the wide field of nature" because it seemed to prove that hybrids could not reproduce themselves.

But Kölreuter continued his experiments.

He examined the pollen of the hybrids and found it shrunken and obviously sterile. He could not tell by looking whether the ovaries were sterile or not. He decided to test the fertility of the hybrid ovaries. He tried fertilizing hybrids with pollen from the parent species *Nicotiana rustica* and *Nicotiana paniculata* which were known to be fertile. The first generation hybrid plant F_1 was crossed with one of the parent plants P_1. The back cross, in some cases, was successful. In such cases, Kölreuter had produced second generation hybrids F_2.

Second generation hybrids can also result from the self-fertilization of hybrids of the first generation or from crosses between them. In the case of the tobacco plants this type of cross could not be made because only the hybrid ovaries were fertile. But when Kölreuter crossed species of pinks *Dianthus*, he got hybrid plants where both pollen and ovaries were fertile. F_1 hybrid *Dianthus* could be crossed to give F_2 hybrid *Dianthus*.

Kölreuter was the first man to make controlled crosses between species of plant and to follow these through two generations and to leave records of his experiments and of his results.

Above Double *Dianthus ruber* (top) and single *Dianthus chinensis* (bottom) which give double flower offspring when crossed. From E. Blackwell *A Curious Herbal*, 1751, and Mrs. Loudon *The Ladies' Flower Garden*, 1840.

His conclusions were that the first generation hybrids were like one another and intermediate between the two parents. He described the hybrid between a red-flower plant and a yellow-flower plant as "of mixed red and yellow. The flowers played into orange-yellow."

There was, however, one exception to intermediacy in Kölreuter's recorded experiments. In crosses between double-flower and single-flower pinks, the hybrids had double flowers. Kölreuter concluded that the pollen from the double flowers had the power of doubling the single ones.

This was the first recorded case in plants of a dominant character. Double flowers were dominant to single flowers. But, as it was the only case Kölreuter found in his experiments, he merely observed it and recorded it. For Kölreuter it was the intermediacy of all the other hybrids that was important.

Kölreuter had found that it did not matter which way round a cross was made: it did not matter which of the parents provided the pollen, which the ovary. He concluded, therefore, that male and female parents both contributed a share of "juices" to the offspring. Juices from the pollen and juices from the ovary combined to give an intermediate juice for the hybrid.

In contrast to the similarity and uniformity of the first generation hybrids, Kölreuter found that second generation hybrids F_2 were not all alike. Although they were made by self-fertilization of the F_1, they had different mixtures of characters and sometimes resembled one of the original parent plants P_1 more than the hybrid parent F_1. From this he concluded that hybrid juices of the F_1 combined in an irregular and unnatural way to give the variety of the F_2 generation.

Kölreuter's experiments were to him evidence of the perfection of Nature. The intermediate F_1 hybrids showed the characters of one parent perfectly blended

Above Joseph Gottlieb Kölreuter.

with those of the other. The breakdown of this perfection in the second generation was because man had interfered and was crossing plants "not intended for one another by the wise Creator."

Kölreuter was writing before Darwin and he believed that his experiments proved that species were fixed. He was writing before the process of fertilization was understood and believed that several pollen grains fertilized the ovary. He was writing before the cell theory and believed that the process of fertilization was a blending of juices.

Kölreuter concluded from his experiments that hybrids did not breed true and, therefore, could not be new species.

The second man mentioned by Mendel in the introduction to his 1866 paper was William Herbert (1788–1847) lawyer and Dean of Manchester. Herbert was interested in the improvement of cultivated flowers and vegetables.

Below Pages from a book by Kölreuter published in 1766. He is describing crosses between varieties of the flower snowflake.

128 ✳✳ ✳ ✳✳

bey dem andern drey Saamenstäubchen genommen hatte, glücklich aufgegangen, und keine geringere Vollkommenheiten, als alle andere, gezeigt haben.

§. 36.

XLIX. Verf.

Levcoj. rubr. ♀.
Levcoj. alb. ♂.

Unter acht aus diesem Versuche erzogenen Pflanzen kamen sechs zur Blüte. Die Blumen waren weißlichtviolet, einfach und vollkommen fruchtbar, und folglich von der in der Fortf. meiner vorläuf. Nachr. S. 45. §. 22. angezeigten Bastartvarietät lediglich nicht unterschieden.

Dritte Fortsetzung

der

vorläufigen Nachricht

von einigen

das Geschlecht der Pflanzen

betreffenden Versuchen

und Beobachtungen,

von

Joseph Gottlieb Kölreuter
der Arzneywissenschaft Doctor, Hochfürstl. Baden-Durlachischen
Rath und Professor der Naturhistorie.

Leipzig,
in der Gleditschischen Handlung,
1766.

Herbert read Kölreuter's work and recognized its importance. He crossed lilies to get new garden varieties and he crossed turnips to improve their cropping qualities. Herbert found that the offspring of crosses between two varieties were often bigger and hardier than either of the parents. Turnip hybrids resembled one parent or the other. They were not intermediates.

Herbert referred to Kölreuter as "the father" of hybridization experiments. He realized that Kölreuter's experiments had been neglected. "They do not seem to have been at all followed up by others or to have attracted the attention of cultivators or botanists as they ought to have done." Like Kölreuter, Herbert was interested in the species problem.

The problem, as Herbert saw it, was a matter of words.

Most botanists of the time believed that, if a cross between two plants that looked different gave rise to fertile offspring under natural conditions, then that proved that the two parents were varieties of the same species. If the offspring from the cross were sterile then that proved that the parents were from different species. If the cross could only be brought about with man's help then that, too, proved they were separate species.

Herbert maintained that, if two plants could be crossed by any means at all to produce offspring, either fertile or sterile, then those two plants were varieties of the same species. Varieties graded into species and it became a matter of convenience where the line was drawn between them.

"Any discrimination," Herbert wrote in 1837, "between species and permanent varieties of plants is artificial, capricious and insignificant; that the question which is perpetually agitated, whether such a wild plant is a new species, or a variety of a known species, is waste of intellect on a point which is capable of no precise definition."

Above The common turnip *Brassica rapa* from J. E. Sowerby *English Botany*, 1873.

36

Mendel's third reference to a predecessor in plant hybridization was to Henri Lecoq (1802–1871).

Lecoq was Director of the Botanic Garden at Clermont-Ferrand in France. He was interested in the techniques of hybridization and in experiment. "However small the corner of the earth may be which a garden amateur can command," Lecoq wrote in 1845, "he is nevertheless in a position to institute a number of useful investigations and noteworthy experiments." He believed that all crop plants could be improved by hybridization and expressed surprise that no one had bred new and more productive varieties of wheat or corn.

Lecoq left detailed descriptions of the practical side of artificial fertilization and he observed, as Kölreuter had done, that "one has almost the certainty of getting many double flowers, as soon as one of the crossed species has become double, and in no wise was the doubleness of both parents necessary as many gardeners believe."

Right Improved wheat (left) and ordinary German field wheat (right) from H. de Vries *The Mutation Theory,* 1910.

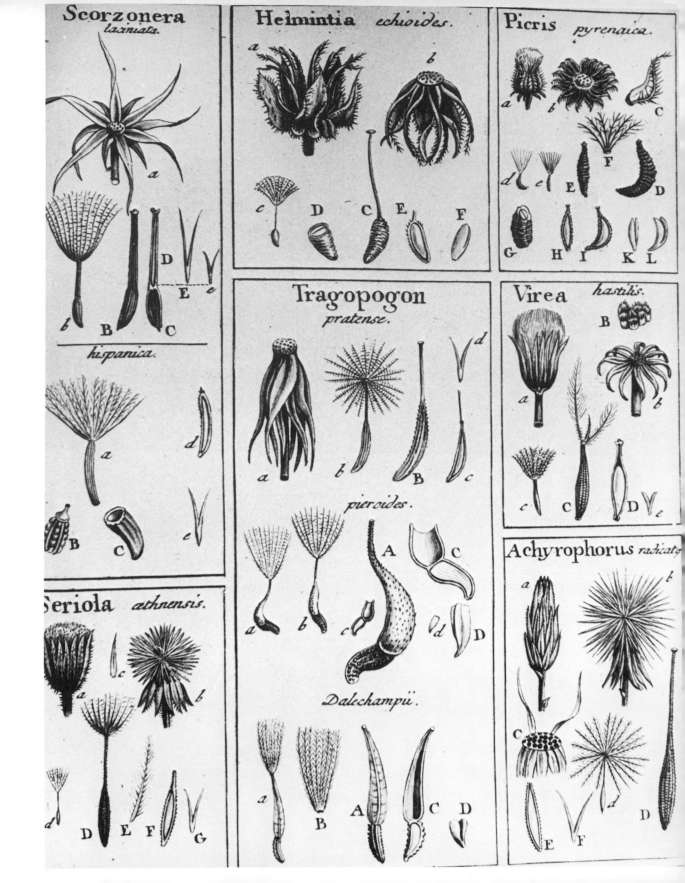

Scorzonera *laciniata.*

hispanica.

Helmintia *echioides.*

Tragopogon *pratense.*

picroides.

Dalechampii.

Picris *pyrenaica.*

Virea *hastilis.*

Achyrophorus *radicata*

Seriola *athnensis.*

Mendel's most important reference was to Karl Friedrich von Gärtner (1772–1850).

Gärtner was a doctor in the village of Calw in the Black Forest about sixty kilometres southeast of Stuttgart. He was the son of a famous botanist who had been a friend of Kölreuter and who had allowed Kölreuter to use his garden for some of his hybridization experiments. When his father died in 1791, Gärtner completed his father's work on the fruiting and seeding of plants.

As a result of this work, Gärtner became fascinated by the problems of hybridization. He decided to investigate these problems. Gärtner inquired into the nature of fertilization in plants and the inheritance of seed colour.

From 1820 to 1840, Gärtner hybridized plants. In 1830, the Dutch Academy of Sciences offered a prize for an answer to the question: *What does experience teach regarding the production of new species and varieties, through the artificial fertilization of flowers of the one with the pollen of the other and what economic and ornamental plants can be produced and multiplied in this way?*

In 1835, Gärtner sent a summary of his work to the Secretary of the Academy. The Academy accepted the entry and Gärtner set about producing a detailed account of his work. In 1837, Gärtner's treatise of two hundred pages with one hundred and fifty hybrid plant specimens won the prize. The treatise was revised and extended to appear, in 1845, with the title *Experiments and Observations on Hybridization in the Plant Kingdom.*

Gärtner's book contained the results of 10,000 experiments in plant hybridization and it was from this book that Mendel obtained the "very valuable observations" of his predecessors in plant hybridization. Mendel's coty of the book is heavily underlined and annotated.

Gärtner classified his hybrids into three types: intermediate, commingled and definite.

Left A page from J. Gärtner *De Fructibus et Semininibus Plantarum*, 1791.

The intermediate type was when a precise balance existed between the fertilizing materials of the parents to give uniform hybrids. The commingled type was intermediate except that the hybrids might show more characters of the one parent than the other. The definite type was when the hybrid resembled only one parent.

Gärtner accounted for his results in terms of the balance of juices. He assumed that one parent's juice might not blend with the other or that the pollen might produce more juice than the ovary. Gärtner, like Kölreuter, did not understand the process of fertilization.

"The general similarity of hybrids with their stem parents," Gärtner wrote, "can be understood by thinking of the seeds as arising from the mixing which occurs in reproduction and not from the pollen alone. However, since very few hybrids show an equal mixing of the characters of both types, but the one factor in the union often preponderates over the other, so the question arises: which laws govern these modifications in the construction of hybrids?"

Gärtner tried to discover the influence of pollen on seed colour in hybrids.

He kept four stocks of maize. One was short with small yellow seeds and the others were tall with large seeds. The large seeds were either brown, red or red-striped. Gärtner tried to cross the short stock with the tall varieties. In 1824, he succeeded with the pollen from the red-striped variety. He got one fertile hybrid plant with five big yellow seeds. The five seeds were sown and Gärtner got four hybrid plants that set seeds. Two had only yellow seeds. One had 224 yellow seeds and 64 red seeds. The other had 104 yellow seeds and 39 red seeds.

Yellow seed to red seed occurred in the proportion of 328 to 103 or 3.18 to 1.

Gärtner worked with the garden pea *Pisum sativum* and recorded the results in the first generation of

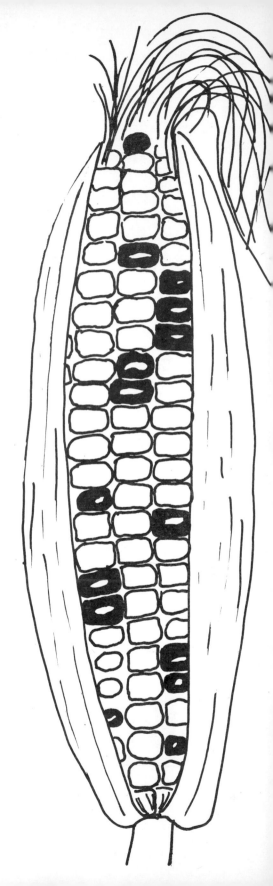

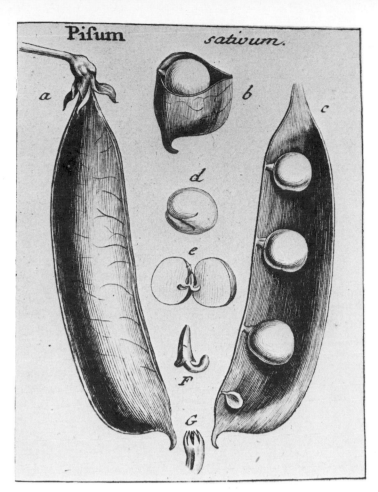

Right The garden pea *Pisum sativum* from J. Gärtner *De Fructibus et Semininibus Plantarum*, 1791.

Left Corn cob with yellow and red seeds to illustrate K. F. von Gärtner's experiment.

crossing different varieties. He found that, when he fertilized six flowers of the creeping pea (yellow seeds) with the pollen of the early green brockel pea (blue-green seeds), he obtained 22 seeds all of which were yellow. He went on to the second hybrid generation by leaving the plants from the 22 seeds to self-fertilize. He obtained some yellow seeds and some blue-green seeds. "The above-mentioned change in colour of the seeds of *Pisum sativum* through hybrid fertilization," Gärtner wrote, "comes out in the second generation more definitely and more decidedly than in the first immediate hybrid product through the immediate influence of the foreign pollen, whereby a quite similar relation as in *Mays* [maize] and other seeds is produced."

41

In contrast to the maize experiments, Gärtner did not record the numbers of yellow and blue-green seeds he got in the second hybrid generation of pea crosses. But he had observed dominant characters in seed colours. Yellow in maize and in the pea had obscured the other colours in the first generation hybrid. But, like Kölreuter, Gärtner merely observed it and recorded it.

Gärtner had got a 3 to 1 ratio for seed colour in second generation maize hybrids. He observed and recorded it.

Like Kölreuter, Gärtner believed in juices. Not only that at fertilization male and female juices blended to give character but also that more than one pollen grain was responsible for fertilization of the ovary.

Like Herbert, Gärtner tried to define a species. But Gärtner believed in the "essentiality" of the species. Varieties that were fertile with one another could not as such be thought of as separate species. There was, according to Gärtner, a "specific form" and a "definite sexual relationship" between species.

Gärtner believed in the fixity of species. The infertility of tobacco plant hybrids was proof of this fixity. "Form and essence," according to Gärtner, "are in this connection one."

Mendel's final reference in his introduction is to another German hybridizer Max Ernst Wichura (1817–1866).

Wichura was a botanist in Breslau. In 1865, he published the results of the work he had been doing on the willow *Salix*. He did not study individual characters of plants, as Gärtner had done, but crossed different species of willow and studied the plants as a whole. He found that many hybrids were bigger and more vigorous than the parental types.

Wichura's hybrids were usually intermediate between the parents. "In hybrid fertilization, if unlike factors unite, there arises an intermediate formation." The same result obtained whichever parent

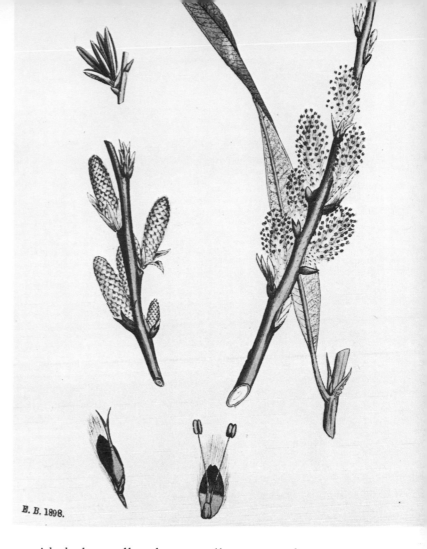

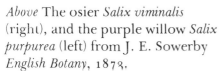

E. B. 1898.

Above The osier *Salix viminalis* (right), and the purple willow *Salix purpurea* (left) from J. E. Sowerby *English Botany*, 1873.

provided the pollen because "constant characters, through which the parent species are distinguished from one another, go half over to the hybrid so that it holds the middle position between them." Wichura's idea of fertilization was more precise than either Kölreuter's or Gärtner's had been.

In referring to reciprocal crosses Wichura states that it follows "with mathematical certainty, that the pollen cell must have exactly the same share in the conformation of the fertilization product as the egg." His writings reflect the growing influence of the cell theory on the interpretation of the process of fertilization.

43

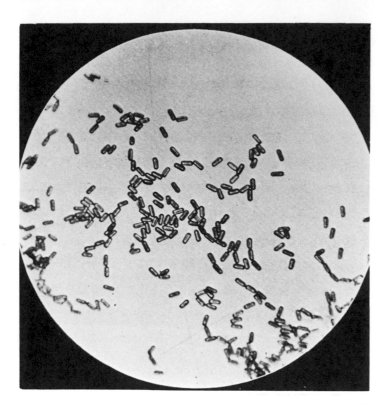

Left Pollen grains (magnified about 68 times) of the garden pea from A. D. Darbishire *Breeding and the Mendelian Discovery,* 1911.

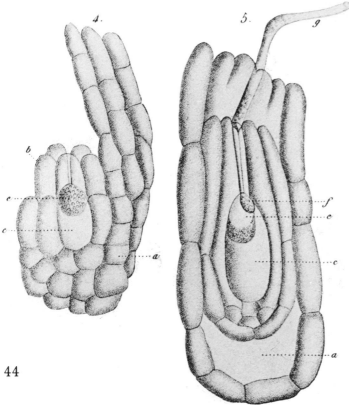

Left Fertilization in an orchid from J-B. Amici *Sur la fécondation des orchidées,* 1847: 4. before fertilization, 5. at the moment of fertilization; f, pollen tube.

Below Fertilization in the green alga *Oedogonium* from N. Pringsheim, 1856.

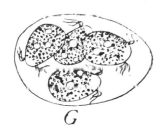

G

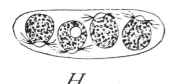

H

Mendel had studied under Franz Unger at Vienna and Unger was a supporter of the 1838 cell theory of Schleiden. Schleiden believed that cells were the basis of all living organisms. But Schleiden was unable to interpret the process of fertilization.

Many years before the cell theory, the Italian microscopist Jean-Baptista Amici (1784–1860) had been able to study a single pollen grain and had watched it put out a projection. In 1830, with an improved microscope, he was able to see the projection from the pollen grow as a tube down the style of a female plant to reach and make contact with the ovary. Watching this in orchids and gourds, he was convinced that only one pollen tube ever grew down to the egg cell and he was also convinced that the pollen tube never penetrated the egg cell. He explained what he saw in the conventional manner of the time. Juice leaked from the end of the pollen tube through the membranes of the ovary to blend with the juices of the egg cell.

Schleiden was opposed to the idea of juices. He was also opposed to the idea of equal contribution by male and female. He thought the beginning of the new plant, the plant embryo, was formed from the tip of the pollen tube where it pushed into the wall of the embryo sac. The embryo sac provided only nourishment for the embryo to develop. He would not accept that there could be a fusion of male pollen and female egg cell elements in spite of the growing evidence of the plant hybridizers.

In 1856, Nathaniel Pringsheim (1823–1894) saw fertilization in the freshwater alga *Oedogonium*. One spermatozoon went into one egg cell. In 1856, a pupil of Schleiden's saw the pollen tube nucleus enter the embryo sac and fuse with the egg cell nucleus.

Schleiden was at last convinced that male and female plants contribute equally to the offspring by the fusion of cells.

In 1856, Mendel began his experiments.

45

5 Mendel's Experiments

Above Mendel in 1862.

Cell theory and a hundred years of experimental hybridization had shown that male and female plants contribute equally to their offspring. Plant hybridizers had studied single characters and recorded dominance. Gärtner had counted coloured maize seeds of the second generation. But no unifying principle of inheritance had been found.

Mendel brought the techniques of physics to the study of plant breeding. The laws of chance and of probability were applied to the process of fertilization. Two cells fuse to give one cell. "It remains, therefore, purely a matter of chance," Mendel wrote, "which of the two sorts of pollen will become united with each separate egg cell."

Design and method from physical experiment was brought into biology. Mendel intended to count the results of hybrid crosses. To count significantly required planned experiments. "Not one" experiment by plant hybridizers "had been carried out to such an extent and in such a way," Mendel wrote, "as to make it possible to determine the number of different forms under which the offspring of hybrids appear, or to arrange these forms with certainty according to their separate generations or definitely to ascertain their statistical relations."

A suitable plant was required that had easily controlled self-fertilization and cross-fertilization so that there should be no difficulty in bringing about one or the other according to the plan of the experiment. It must be easy to protect the flowers from unwanted pollen. Mendel chose the pea family because of the structure of the flowers.

The stamens and style are packed inside the keel, formed from the fusion of the two lower petals. Self-

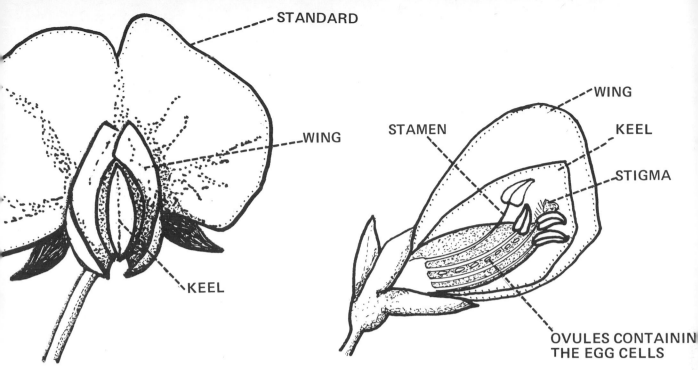

STANDARD

WING

KEEL

WING

STAMEN

KEEL

STIGMA

OVULES CONTAININ
THE EGG CELLS

Above Diagram of a pea flower.

fertilization takes place inside this package before the flower opens. Self-fertilization, therefore, usually occurs before there is any possibility of pollen from other plants reaching the stigma.

Cross-fertilization would be done by hand. "For this purpose," Mendel wrote, "the bud is opened before it is perfectly developed, the keel is removed and each stamen carefully extracted by means of forceps, after which the stigma can at once be dusted over with the foreign pollen." The flowers would then be covered with a bag.

From among the plants that have this type of flower in the pea family, Mendel selected the garden pea *Pisum sativum*. Many varieties were obtainable and they were easy to grow. The peas were grown on a small garden plot behind the monastery building. To keep several experiments going at the same time, the plants were crammed together growing over the fence and up trees. When there was no more room on the plot, which was the only part of the garden he was allowed to use for his experiments, the peas could be grown in pots.

Plants suitable for Mendel's experiments had to have conspicuous characters that stayed constant in self-fertilizing lines. Each variety of pea was cultivated and allowed to self-fertilize for two years. All but one remained constant where each generation was like the last. Mendel had established pure lines that proved not to vary.

From thirty-four varieties of pea, Mendel selected twenty-two that had characters that were easy to study. During the period of experiments, from 1856 to 1863, the twenty-two varieties were allowed to grow and self-fertilize. Thus, Mendel always had a standard to which he could refer the results of his artificial crossings.

Above The garden where Mendel grew his peas. His rooms were on the first floor above the garden. Tall and short pea plants have been planted in the garden.

Above left Tall and short pea seedlings sown at the same time.

Above right Yellow and green pod pea plants from A. D. Darbishire *Breeding and the Mendelian Discovery*, 1911.

Plants grown in a greenhouse served as controls for the outdoor crosses. Bees and weevils could be kept out of the greenhouse so there was no risk of cross-fertilization by these animals. This was the first time that experiments in plant hybridization had been planned in this way.

Plants suitable for Mendel's experiments had to have contrasting characters. He found several characters of form and size and colour that had simple alternatives in the pure breeding lines. Mendel selected fifteen characters but, finally, reduced the number to the seven that showed the clearest contrasts.

He found it difficult to make a decision between a

small pea and a big pea, a small leaf and a big leaf because, as he wrote, "the difference is of a *more or less* nature." He rejected the "more or less" characters and chose to study colour and form of flowers, pods and seeds. Length of stem was also included because it proved not to be a "more or less" character. Long stemmed plants were six times taller than short stemmed plants.

Mendel crossed plants with purple flowers and brown seed coats with plants with white flowers and white seed coats after proving that the colour of the seed coat and of the flowers was always the same on the one plant.

Above The brothers of the monastery 1861–1864. Mendel is third from the right holding a fuchsia flower. Abbot Napp is fourth from the right.

50

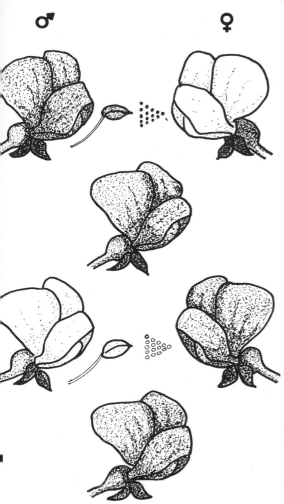

♂ ♀

Above Reciprocal crosses between purple flower and white flower varieties of the garden pea. In the top cross the purple flower plant provides pollen, in the bottom cross the white flower plant provides pollen.

He crossed plants with flowers evenly distributed along the stalk with plants with flowers clustered at the tip. He crossed plants with smooth seeds with plants with wrinkled seeds. He crossed plants with yellow or orange seeds with plants with seeds of a "more or less intense green tint." He crossed plants with fat pods with plants with shrunk pods. He crossed plants with green pods with plants with yellow or red pods. He crossed plants with long stems (over two metres) and plants with short stems (under half a metre).

Mendel used only the plants in which the characters were conspicuous and contrasting.

He always made two sets of crosses: one variety provided the pollen for the first cross; the other variety provided it for the second.

Mendel said that he knew already from what he had seen of ornamental plants that hybrids are not always exactly intermediate between the parents. They may, for example, be intermediate in the form and size of the leaves but in other characters one of the two parental characters is "preponderant." Mendel now showed that in none of his crosses with the seven selected characters were the offspring intermediate between the parents.

Mendel proposed to call the character that preponderated the dominant character and the other, that did not show in the hybrids, the recessive.

He selected plants for the experiments which showed clear dominance relationships. He had, in fact, purposely rejected those characters, such as size of seed and leaf, that showed a range of intermediacy in the hybrids.

When Mendel crossed a plant with purple flowers with a plant with white flowers, all the offspring had purple flowers. It did not matter which was the pollen-producing plant. Purple was dominant to white. There were no intermediate plants with pink flowers.

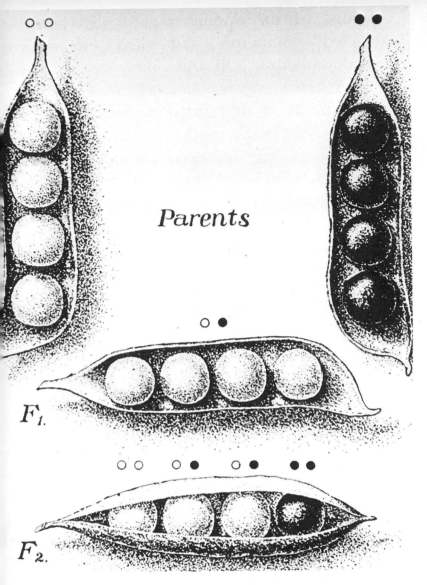

Parents

F₁.

F₂.

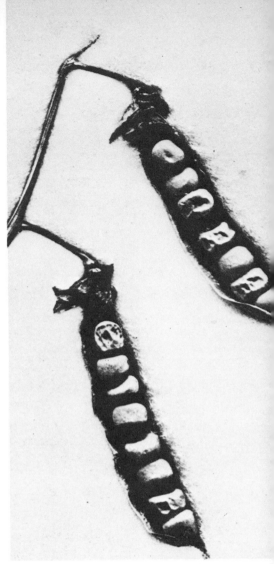

Kölreuter saw this in his crosses of double and single pinks. Gärtner's yellow-seed maize was dominant to his red-seed maize. But Kölreuter and Gärtner had observed and recorded only unrelated facts.

Of the other six characters, Mendel found that even distribution of flowers was dominant to clustered. The smooth pea was dominant to the wrinkled pea and the yellow pea to the green pea. The fat pod was dominant to the shrunk pod and the green pod to the yellow pod. Finally, Mendel found that the tall stem was dominant to the short stem.

Herbert observed that his hybrid turnips were

Above left Inheritance of yellow and green pea colour from E. G. Conklin *Heredity and Environment*, 1922.

Above Inheritance of round and wrinkled seeds in pea plants from A. D. Darbishire *Breeding and the Mendelian Discovery*, 1911.

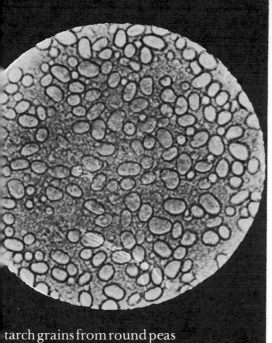

tarch grains from round peas
bove) and wrinkled peas (below);
e irregular shape and size of
rains, as well as the small number,
re responsible for the wrinkling of
e pea.
rom A. D. Darbishire *Breeding and the
endelian Discovery,* 1911.

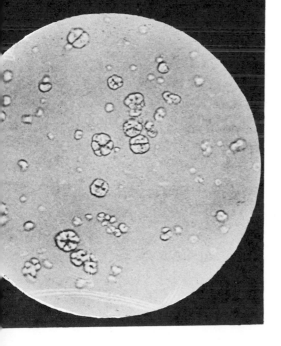

bigger and hardier than the parents. Wichura's hybrid willows were bigger and more vigorous. Mendel observed that the hybrid between a tall plant and a short plant was often taller than the tall parent.

In *Experiments in Plant Hybridization,* Mendel described these experiments and concluded that Kölreuter and Gärtner were wrong in saying that almost all first generation hybrids were intermediate between the two parents. "Transitional forms," he wrote, "were not observed in any experiment." Instead, Mendel argued that one character was usually dominant to the other and the hybrid, therefore, resembled only one of its parents.

Mendel continued to the second generation.

The hybrid from a cross between a plant with smooth peas and one with wrinkled peas had smooth peas only.

Mendel let 253 smooth pea hybrids self-fertilize. The result was 7,324 peas. Mendel found that 5,474 of the peas were smooth but 1,850 were wrinkled.

Smooth was dominant to wrinkled and all the F_1 generation hybrids had smooth peas. But in the F_2 generation the wrinkled turned up again. In the experiment the count gave a proportion of 2.96 smooth peas to 1 wrinkled.

Other hybrid self-fertilizations gave similar results in the F_2 generation.

Yellow peas occurred in the proportion of 3.01 dominant yellow peas to 1 recessive green pea. 787 tall plants occurred with 277 short pea plants, 2.84 to 1. 705 plants with purple flowers occurred with 224 plants with white flowers, 3.15 to 1.

Mendel discovered constant relationships between the dominant and recessive characters in the second hybrid generation. A relationship of three plants with the dominant character to one plant with the recessive. Mendel concluded that the characters "must pass over [from one generation to the next] unchanged."

The next stage was to see what happened when the plants of the second hybrid generation self-fertilized.

The hybrids that showed the recessive character bred true. All the offspring had green peas or were short or had white flowers. But only one third of the dominant character bearing plants bred true.

The yellow-pea hybrids and the tall hybrids and the purple-flower hybrids bred one-third true and the other two-thirds behaved like the hybrids of the Fi generation and produced plants some of which showed the dominant characters and some the recessive in the proportion of 3 to 1.

Mendel confirmed the findings of Gärtner and Kölreuter that hybrids often revert to the parental forms but Mendel's interpretation of the results was revolutionary.

To explain his results, he considered each of the characters as a unitary unchanging character. "If A be taken as denoting one of the two constant characters, for instance, the dominant, a the recessive, and Aa the hybrid form in which both are conjoined, the expression $A + 2Aa + a$ shows the terms in the series of progeny of the hybrids of two differentiating characters." The hybrid Aa possesses both the characters of the parents but appears to be only like the parent with the dominant character.

He then argues that the hybrid produces pollen or egg cells that are either A or a and in equal numbers. "In the opinion of renowned physiologists, for the purpose of propagation one pollen cell and one egg cell unite in phanerogams [plants that produce seeds] into a single cell, which is capable of assimilation and formation of new cells to become an independent organism." He supposed that it would be entirely a matter of chance whether an A pollen grain fertilized an A egg cell or an a egg cell and illustrated the point with the following diagram.

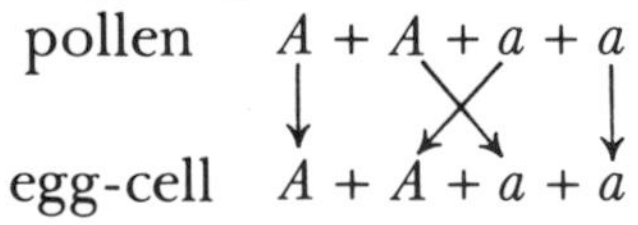

$$\text{pollen} \quad A + A + a + a$$
$$\text{egg-cell} \quad A + A + a + a$$

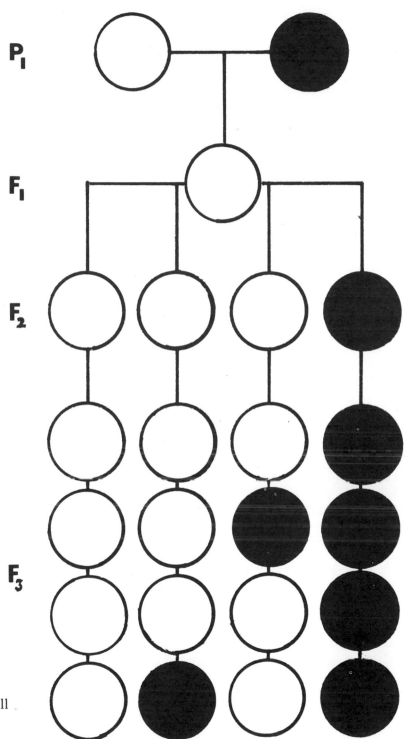

Right Inheritance of yellow and green peas through three filial generations. After the first cross all the plants are self-fertilized.

Mendel not only explained the facts of hybridization through three generations but also confirmed mathematically that the contributions of pollen and egg cell were equal. He suggested that characters occur in pairs with dominance relations to one another. He decided on mathematical grounds that each parent passes on only one of its two characters to its offspring and this character combines with only one of the characters of the other parent.

This is called *Mendel's First Law* or the *Law of Segregation*. The revolutionary part of this work was to suggest unchanging factors existing in pairs but which segregated (separated) from one another so that only one character of the pair was contained in the pollen grain and only one in the egg cell. The two single characters then united to give the pairs for the next generation. The characters from the two parents did not blend nor alter one another in any way. They were there unchanged and ready to segregate again to give new combinations in the F_2 generation.

Which character combines with which at fertilization is a matter of chance but according to "the laws of probability," Mendel wrote, "it will always happen, on the average of many cells, that each pollen from A and a will unite equally often with each egg cell from A and a." By the operation of the law of chance the types will appear in the F_2 generation in the proportion of $AA + 2Aa + aa$ or three apparent dominant types to one recessive.

In 1861, Mendel tried crossing plants that differed from one another in more than one character. Again, he did not find intermediate forms. He crossed plants that had smooth peas which were yellow with plants that had wrinkled seeds which were green. The first generation were all with smooth and yellow peas because these two characters are dominant. When he allowed eighteen of these hybrids to self-fertilize, he managed to get 556 peas. 315 were smooth and yellow, 101 were wrinkled and yellow, 108 were

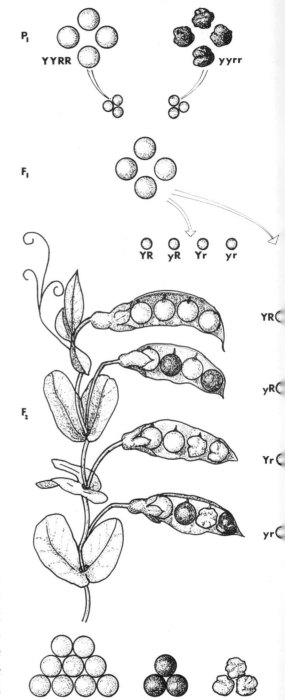

Above Mendel with part of an excursion group that visited Paris and London in 1862.

Left Inheritance of two independent characters in *Pisum sativum*, yellow and green, round and wrinkled.

smooth and green and 32 were wrinkled and green.

From this, Mendel concluded that the characters were segregating and combining independently of one another because this ratio for two characters, $9 + 3 + 3 + 1$, is the product of the simple multiplication of the results from each pair of characters separately $(3 + 1) \times (3 + 1)$.

This finding is known as *Mendel's Second Law* or the *Law of Independent Assortment*.

In 1865, Mendel talked about his results to the Brno Natural History Society. The local newspaper reported the "interesting" work. Society members, local teachers and doctors, were stimulated to a "brief" discussion.

In addition to peas, Mendel talked about beans and pinks. He found that white-flower or red-flower clove pinks *Dianthus caryophyllus* bred true. Mendel had crossed runner beans *Phaseolus multiflorus* and French beans *Phaseolus vulgaris* with the bush bean *Phaseolus nanus*.

In beans, Mendel showed that height, pod colour

Above The clove pink *Dianthus caryophyllus* from J. Baxter *British Phanerogamous Botany*, 1835–1843.

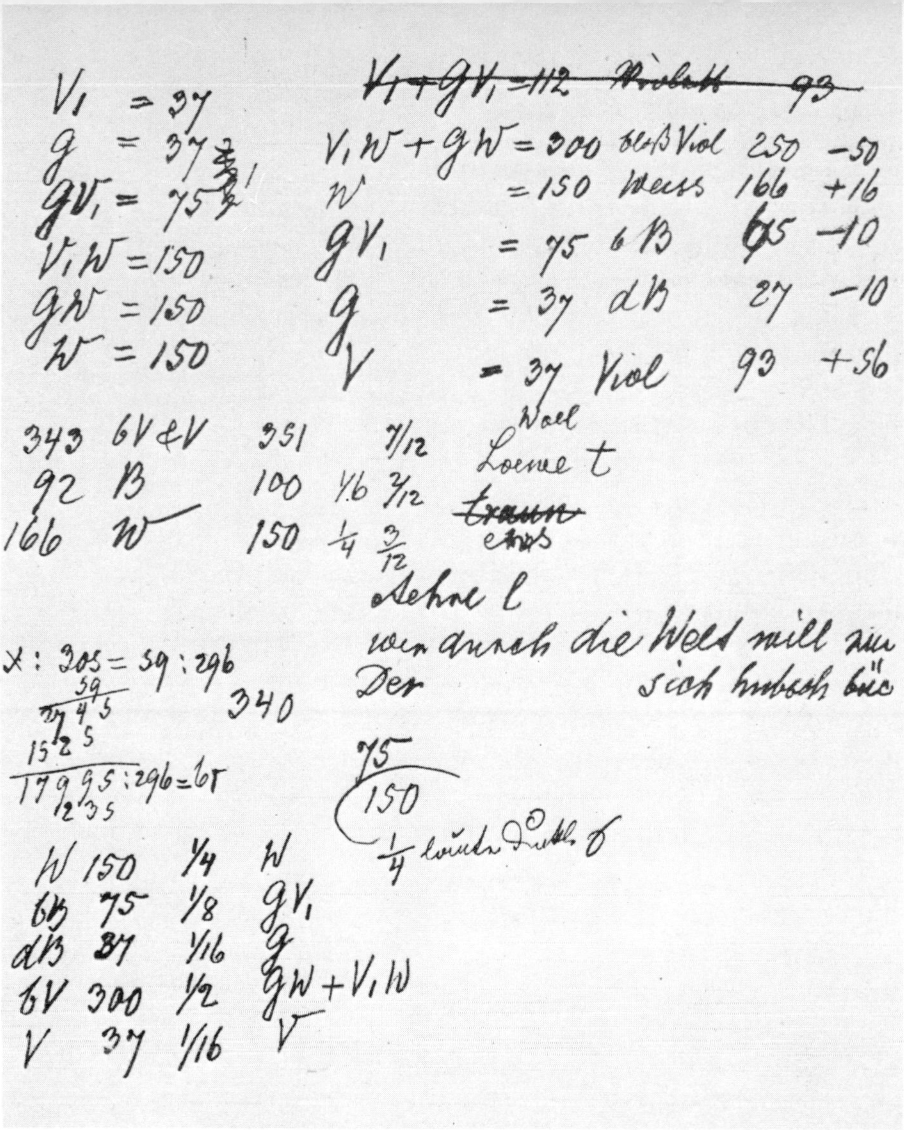

$V_1 = 37$

$g = 37\frac{1}{2}$

$gV_1 = 75\frac{1}{2}$

$V_1W = 150$

$gW = 150$

$W = 150$

$V_1 + gV_1 = 112$ Violett   93

$V_1W + gW = 300$ dunkl Viol   250 -50

$W = 150$ Weiss   166 $+16$

$gV_1 = 75$ hB   65 -10

$g = 37$ dB   27 -10

$V = 37$ Viol   93 $+56$

343	bV & V	351	7/12
92	B	100	4.6 3/12
166	W	150	1/4 3/12

Noel

Loewe t

~~braun~~ etws

Aehre l

wer durch die Welt will zu

Der   sich hübsch bie

$X : 305 = 59 : 296$

59

340

$15 \cdot 2 \cdot 5$

$179.95 : 296 = 65$

$\frac{75}{150}$ $\frac{1}{4}$ etc

W	150	1/4	W
bB	75	1/8	gV_1
dB	37	1/16	g
bV	300	1/2	$gW + V_1W$
V	37	1/16	V

Above Some of Mendel's notes on crosses he made between different sorts of beans.

and pod form were characters inherited in exactly the same way as in the pea. But flower colour proved difficult. Mendel was puzzled because a cross between a plant with red flowers and one with white flowers resulted in offspring with red flowers paler than the red parent.

When Mendel let this F_1 generation self-fertilize, the F_2 gave every variety of flower colour from red to white. Pure white was rare. Mendel suggested that flower colour in beans must be controlled by more than one character.

Mendel assumed that all hybrid plants should

follow the rules for *Pisum*. Gärtner's intermediate hybrids could be the result either of studying many characters at the same time, not all of which were dominant in the same parent; the result of not making pure lines first; or the result of having features which, like the bean flower colours, were the result of several interacting characters. Much of the confusion in hybrid crosses, according to Mendel, was because in the F$_2$ generation the apparent dominants did not all behave in the same way when self-fertilized. He distinguished two types among the apparent dominants.

Mendel was the first to distinguish between the outward appearance of a plant (now called the phenotype) and the inward composition (now called the genotype). The three dominant purple-flower peas of the F$_2$ generation were all of the same phenotype. They were not all of the same genotype. One third had two like characters *PP* the other two-thirds had two unlike characters *Pp*.

Below Two pea plants of the same phenotype, purple flower and tall, but different genotypes.

Mendel realized that large numbers are needed to give meaningful results. The number required increases as the number of characters being studied increases. Mendel criticized Gärtner for not having used enough plants in his crosses.

Mendel did not think that either Gärtner or Kölreuter had proved by their experiments that species were fixed. Neither did he think that his own experiments proved that they were not. But "changes of type must take place if the conditions of life be altered and the species possesses the capacity of fitting itself to its new environment." Like Herbert, Mendel thought that species and varieties graded into one another.

"It has so far been found," Mendel wrote, "to be just as impossible to draw a sharp line between hybrids of species and varieties as between species and varieties themselves."

In 1866, Mendel's contribution to the Brno Natural History Society was published. Mendel received forty reprints of *Experiments in Plant Hybridization*. He is known to have sent out several copies one of which went to Karl Wilhelm von Nägeli.

Nägeli (1817–1891) had worked with Schleiden in Jena and had shown that cells were formed from other cells by dividing in half and not by budding as Schleiden and others believed. In 1865, Nägeli had published a review of the work of Kölreuter and Gärtner. Nägeli agreed with Mendel, rather than with the others, that there was no great difference between species and varieties except that varieties were more like one another and tended to be more fertile, but he followed Kölreuter and Gärtner in thinking that the F_1 generation was the result of an unknown type of mixing of the parent characters to give a new hybrid character.

Further, Nägeli believed that all the individuals of later generations must be variable. There was no suggestion to his mind that half the F_2 generation

Below Karl Wilhelm Nägeli.

could breed true (either for the dominant characters or the recessives). When Nägeli received Mendel's paper he could not believe that Mendel had found the answer to the inheritance of characters in plant hybrids.

Nägeli believed that all hybrid plants of both F_1 and F_2 generations would have both *A* and *a* in their bodies and sooner or later this hybrid condition would show itself. Nägeli was working with the hawkweeds *Hieracium* and his hybrids bred true. Not unnaturally, his reply to Mendel's paper was to suggest that Mendel should do some work with *Hieracium*.

Right Florets of *Hieracium pilosella* from J. E. Sowerby *English Botany*, 1873.

Right The creeping, or mouse-ear, hawkweed *Hieracium pilosella* from J. Hill *The Vegetable System*, 1777.

Left First page of the manuscript of *Experiments in Plant Hybridization* by G. Mendel, 1865.

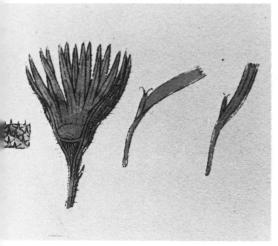

The hawkweeds are very difficult to cross because of the arrangement of the reproductive parts of the flower. Each floret has a fine tube, formed by the fusion of the stamens, through which the style passes. It needs delicate dissection and good eyesight to remove the stamens without damaging the style.

Mendel tried to improve the lighting conditions for this operation by using an artificial light source with a lens and mirrors but suffered severe eye strain.

Mendel worked on *Hieracium* for five years, from 1866 to 1871, and he could not get the same results as he had got with *Pisum*. Most of his crosses were a failure but when he did succeed in making fertile hybrids they bred true, to his surprise. In 1869, Mendel read a paper on *Hieracium* to the Brno Natural History Society.

He could not explain his results but it is clear that he still considered that *Pisum* illustrated the usual way of inheritance and that *Hieracium*, like the willows of Wichura, showed "peculiar behaviour of their hybrids." In this Mendel was correct.

Hawkweed is an example of a plant that reproduces by apomixis. That is to say, the pollen only stimulates the egg cell to develop, it does not fuse with it. This makes it difficult to make crosses in the first place and, because there is no fertilization in the normal reproductive process, the hybrids do indeed breed true.

It is not surprising that Mendel was unable to explain *Hieracium* nor very surprising that Nägeli thought Mendel was wrong about the F_2 hybrid generation showing segregation into pure types like the P_1 generation and hybrid types like the F_1.

From a piece of paper with Mendel's writing on it, it is known that he was still trying to work out a common law of heredity for the *Hieracium*, *Salix* and *Pisum* results in the late 1870s.

But, by 1866, Mendel's contributions to biological theory were finished.

6 *Mendel the Abbot*

In 1868, the local newspaper of Brno announced the election of a new abbot. Abbot Napp died and the twelve brothers elected Mendel to succeed him. "The population," the local newspaper reported, "greets the election with undivided joy."

In a letter to Nägeli, Mendel expressed the hope that, as abbot, he would have more time and, more important, more space.

He resigned from teaching at the Technical School. But, as abbot of a rich and influential monastery, Mendel was expected to play a part in local politics. In 1872, Mendel was made Commander of the Order of Franz Joseph for his "meritorious and patriotic activities" as abbot.

Right One of Mendel's microscopes, one of his magnifying glasses and his spectacles.

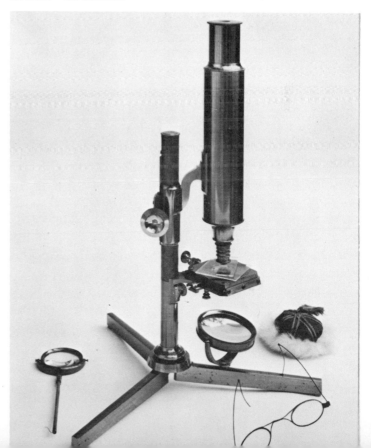

Left Abbot Mendel.

In politics, Mendel supported the German Liberal Party and, when the Party was asked to propose a chairman for the Moravian Mortgage Bank, Mendel was appointed. The chairmanship meant daily duties at the Bank. Mendel was elected to committees on education, on roads, on agriculture. He had to manage the monastery estates and visit farms. Mendel had the whole monastery garden for his experiments but he had less time.

But, until 1871, Mendel went on with the *Hieracium* experiments. The experiments were difficult and the results unsatisfactory. Finally, increasing calls on his time persuaded him to abandon *Hieracium*.

Mendel made few further planned experiments but he did satisfy himself from fertilization experiments with the marvel of Peru *Mirabilis jalapa* that one pollen grain was enough for fertilization. He saw that fertilization was often more successful if there were a number of grains on the stigma. Mendel put this down to a rivalry that existed between the grains so that only the most vigorous succeeded.

Above The bee house in the
monastery garden.

Mendel's scientific work became a leisure activity.

He set up colonies of bees and designed a fertilization cage to control crosses between bees of different
varieties. He obtained bees from Italy, Carinthia and
Cyprus as well as South American bees that arrived in
Moravia in a load of timber. He gave lectures to the
Brno Natural History Society on bee-keeping and
bee-breeding.

Unfortunately, none of Mendel's research notes on
bees has survived.

Mendel observed that a hive from which the queen
had been taken rears more of its own queens even if
supplied immediately with a queen of another variety.
Mendel studied the inheritance of the industry of the
hive, flight characteristics, bee colour and readiness to
sting. No results survive. It has been suggested that
one of Mendel's aims was to test the observation,
made in 1854, that the drones produced by a hybrid
queen resemble either of her parents but are never
intermediate.

Mendel grafted and hybridized fruit trees and

flowers. He established, by crossing, pear strains that ripened at different times of the year. He displayed the results of his breeding experiments at local agricultural shows. He won prizes and a fuchsia was named after him. The "Prelate Mendel" was "very large, pale blue shading into violet, luxuriant, regular structure, sepals light, very beautiful, blooms early." The fuchsia was Mendel's favourite flower and he put one into his coat of arms.

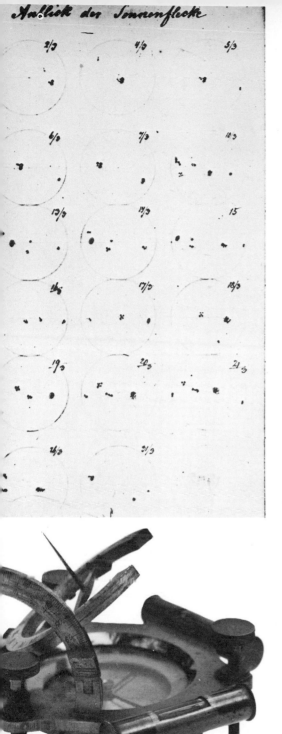

Anblick der Sonnenflecke

Every day, Mendel made recordings of air pressure, temperature and hours of sunshine. He summed up the material in monthly graphs. He studied sun spots.

In another paper to the Brno Natural History Society, he came to the conclusion that there was a relation between sunspot activity and the northern lights *aurora borealis* and a relation between the eleven-year sunspot cycle and the weather. Others have had the same idea but, because it seemed unlikely that sun spots as such could alter the climate, the idea has always been rejected. A new theory, however, of climate controlled by the earth's magnetic field has brought sun spots back.

The link between the sunspot cycle and the weather in the northern hemisphere has been confirmed. It has been suggested that the electrically-charged particles from the sun interact with particles from the earth's magnetic field. This, it seems, affects the circulation of the atmosphere and, thus, the weather.

Mendel's health deteriorated. He became involved in political disputes. The government proposed a heavy tax on Church property to raise money to support parish priests. The monastery of Brno refused to pay. Mendel considered the State was interfering in the internal affairs of Rome. He exhausted himself with ten years of legal battles over the tax.

On 6th January, 1884, Mendel died of Bright's disease: chronic deterioration of the kidneys.

While abbot, Mendel found time to provide for his sisters' sons. Theresia gave up her dowry for her brother's education. Mendel sent his nephews to school in Brno and then to Vienna University to read medicine.

"His death," the local newspaper reported, "deprives the poor of a benefactor and mankind at large of a man of the noblest character, one who was a warm friend, a promoter of the natural sciences and an exemplary priest."

7 Plant Hybridization and Cell Theory after Mendel

There were no immediate successors to Mendel.

In 1866, the Brno Natural History Society sent six copies of its *Transactions* to Vienna, eight to Berlin, four to the United States and two to England. Some of Mendel's reprints have been traced. He sent one to Holland, one to the Austrian botanist Anton Kerner von Marilaun (1831–1898) and two to Germany, one of which was the copy to Nägeli in Munich. But, in 1866, Mendel's paper aroused little interest.

Nägeli, for example, was not prepared to publicize Mendel's experiments because they did not explain the results of his own experiments. Authors of books on plant hybridization were mainly interested in the hawkweed paper. No one suspected that Mendel's results had universal application.

But Mendel's mathematical approach to plant hybridization had provided a vigorous new theory. Hereditary units, or particles, exist in pairs. Each unit separates from its partner and passes by itself into a germ cell. This is known as segregation. When male and female germ cells fuse in sexual reproduction each unit pairs with a new partner and this is known as recombination.

In 1866, there was no physical basis for supposing that characters were in pairs in organisms nor any basis to account for their segregation.

Also, Mendel had not joined his theory with Darwin's theory of evolution by natural selection. Mendel had read Darwin and believed that a continuous evolutionary process was a possibility and that his own work might have some bearing on the problem of the origin of species. "It requires indeed some courage," he wrote of his experiments, "to undertake a labour of such far-reaching extent; this appears, however, to be the only right way by which we can finally reach the solution of a question the importance of which cannot be overestimated in connection with the history of the evolution of organic forms." Apart from this, Mendel did not enter the discussions on evolution.

There is no evidence that Darwin read Mendel's paper. It has been said that if he had, Darwin would have recognized Mendel's importance. The Mendelian theory was what Darwin was looking for as the basis for the variability on which natural selection could work.

But Charles Darwin (1809–1882) knew about the inheritance of recessive characters. He had made experiments with grey and white mice. The offspring were not piebald or pale grey but dark grey like one parent and, in the next generation, were either grey or white. He had crossed hairy and smooth plants and all the plants were hairy, yet smooth ones turned up again in later generations.

Darwin did not believe that these crosses told him anything relevant to evolutionary theory. The "sports" (white mice, for example) would already have been eliminated by natural selection and it was only the artificiality of the crosses that caused them to show up again. A hairy plant was often considered to be a different species from a smooth one and species crosses, according to Darwin, were not the sort of crosses that occurred naturally. If they did occur they did not make a new species.

Finally, Darwin believed in blending inheritance and he also believed that more than one pollen grain grew down the style of a plant to fertilize the egg cell. Blending inheritance depends on the assumptions that each parent contributes equally to the offspring (which agrees with Mendel's theory) and that those contributions are halved at each generation (which does not agree with Mendel's theory). It was Galton, a cousin of Darwin, who worked out blending in-

Below Darwin's mice.

heritance, mathematically, in his *Ancestral Law of Inheritance*.

Francis Galton (1822–1911) thought he could show, from the statistical analysis of populations, that the parent contributes half its inheritance to the offspring (which agrees with Mendel) but that each grandparent provides a quarter and each great-grandparent an eighth of the inheritance (which does not agree with Mendel).

It can be guessed then that Darwin would not have appreciated fully the importance of Mendel's work for the general theory of evolution. It is perhaps not surprising, therefore, that Darwin's followers did not recognize Mendel's work either.

Only three years after the publication of *Experiments in Plant Hybridization*, Mendel's name was recorded in the literature of hybridization. In a book published in Giessen in 1869 on the subject of species and varieties, Hermann Hoffmann (1819–1891) referred twice to Mendel's work, once to some work on *Geum* and once to *Pisum*. Of the *Pisum* work he concludes that Mendel had shown that "hybrids possess an inclination in the following generation to strike back to the parental species."

In 1881, Wilhelm Olbers Focke (1834–1922) published a long work on plant hybridization in which he tried to record all the examples of hybrid plants that had ever been made. He had done some experiments himself on foxgloves and a few other plants and was exceptional in that he recorded the measurements he had made of parts of plants whose inheritance he was studying. He measured the petals and sepals of parent foxgloves and their hybrid offspring and found the hybrid measurements more or less intermediate between the parents. Focke mentions Mendel's work fifteen times but, interestingly, the *Pisum* experiments are mentioned only once, the *Hieracium* work several times. The results of the *Pisum* experiments were not in agreement with other

Below Top: blending inheritance according to Galton; bottom: particulate inheritance according to Mendel.

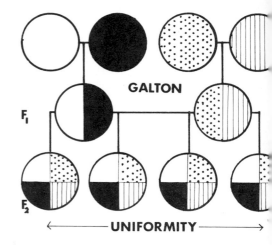

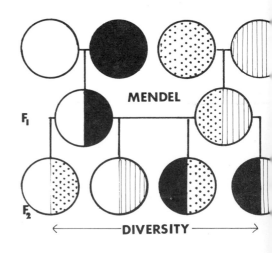

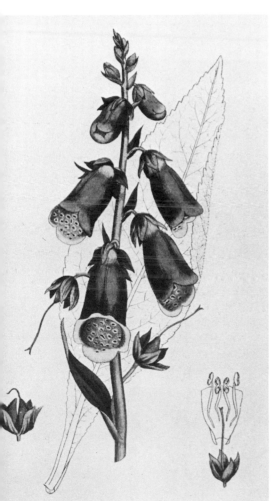

Pisum.

Lit.: Th. A. Knight in Philos. Trans. 1799, II p. 195; **Trans. Hort. Soc. London** V p. 379; Gärtner Bast. S. 316; Darwin Variiren I Cap. 9, 11; Kreuz- u. Selbst befr. S. 151; G. Mendel in Verh. naturf. Ver. Brünn IV Abh. p. 3 ff.

Die ursprüngliche Heimath der Erbse und ihre wilde Stammform sind nicht bekannt. Man findet sie in einer grossen Zahl von Sorten oder Varietäten, von welchen indess zwei oder drei entschieden als die verbreitetsten und ausgezeichnetsten hervorgehoben werden können.

1. *P. sativum sphaerospermum* (*P. sativum L.*): Wuchs niedrig oder mittelhoch, Nebenblätter am Grunde weiss gezeichnet, Blüthe weiss, Samen kugelrund, rollend, gelblich.

2. *P. sativum arvense* (*P. arvense L.*): Wuchs hoch, Nebenblätt am Grunde roth gezeichnet; Fahne der Blüthen roth, Flügel purpur Samen gross, seitlich zusammengedrückt, fast von der Gestalt ei

experiments on hundreds of different plants. Thus, finally, Focke considers Mendel's work as no more than "to be designated as particularly instructive" along with that of several other people.

In the same year, Mendel's name was listed among plant hybridizers in an article that George Romanes (1848–1894) wrote for the *Encyclopaedia Britannica* on *Hybridism*.

In 1895, *Plant Breeding* by Liberty Hyde Bailey (1858–1954) contained no reference to Mendel but, in later editions, quoted Mendel's experiments from Focke's book.

As far as is known, these were the only references to Mendel's work before 1900.

Mendel had been dead sixteen years when the Dutchman Hugo de Vries (1848–1935) sent a paper in March 1900 to the Academy of Sciences in Paris called *On the Law of Segregation in Hybrids*. The conclusion of this short paper was that inheritance could be considered as depending on distinct units that segregate from one another in hybrids. "The totality of these experiments establishes the law of segregation of hybrids and confirms the principles that I have expressed concerning the specific characters considered as being distinct units." At that moment a Dutch friend sent de Vries a copy of Mendel's paper from Delft. "I know that you are studying hybrids"

Left Hugo de Vries.

wrote his friend Professor Martinus Willem Beyerinck (1851–1931), "so perhaps the enclosed reprint of the year 1865 of a certain Mendel which I happen to possess is still of some interest to you." Professor Beyerinck recognized the radical importance of Mendel's work and, at that moment, so did de Vries.

In the German version of his paper which he was just sending off for publication, de Vries hastily altered the conclusion that he had sent to Paris. "From these and many other experiments I conclude that the law of segregation of hybrids in the plant kingdom, which Mendel established for peas, has a very general application and a fundamental significance for the study of the units out of which the specific characters are compounded." De Vries described Mendel's paper as *trop beau pour son temps* "ahead of its time" which accords with Mendel's own disappointed *mein Zeit wird schon kommen* "my time will come".

De Vries was more in touch with the scientific world than Mendel had been and sent reprints of his paper to those it would most affect like Tschermak and Correns.

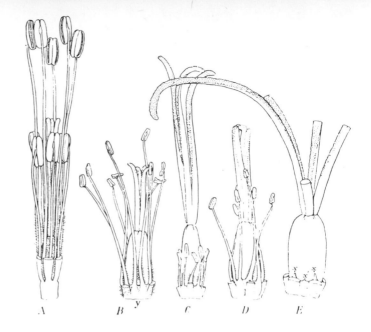

Right Stamens and styles from campion crosses from C. Correns *Die Bestimmung und Vererbung des Geschlechtes*, 1907.
A. *Silene viscosa,* the sticky catchfly.
E. *Silene alba.*
B, C, D. hybrids between the two.

In October 1899, Carl Correns (1864–1933) suddenly had the idea of particulate inheritance and, only a few weeks later, picked up a reference to Mendel's paper in Focke's book. This was not the first time he had heard of Mendel for Correns had been a pupil of Nägeli and Nägeli had mentioned Mendel's work on *Hieracium* but not on peas. In May 1900, a work by Correns appeared called *G. Mendel's Law of the Behaviour of the Progeny of Hybrid Races.*

But Correns realized he had been forestalled by de Vries. The reprint was an immediate stimulus to publication. Correns, forestalled by de Vries, told the world that both of them had been forestalled by Mendel.

Erich von Tschermak (1871–1962) had chosen to study inheritance in peas and, in 1899, searching through the literature, found a reference in Focke's book to the work of Mendel on *Pisum sativum.* "I had on the same day of this discovery the Transactions of the Natural History Society of Brno hunted out of the University Library, which now gave me the information, to my greatest surprise, that the regular relationships discovered by me, had already been discovered by Mendel much earlier." In June 1900, having received his reprint from de Vries, Tschermak published his paper *On Experimental Crosses in Pisum sativum*.

William Bateson (1861–1926) received a reprint of de Vries's paper. He, too, hunted out the 1866 Transactions of the Brno Natural History Society. In May 1900, Bateson lectured to members of the Royal Horticultural Society in London on Mendel's work.

Thus, between 1866 and 1900, three investigators, independently, arrived at laws of inheritance and at a level of understanding where they recognized the full importance of Mendel's work.

This understanding came from developments in cell theory. Apart from Darwin's theory of natural selection, the most spectacular advances in biological studies in the second part of the nineteenth century was in the understanding of the structure and behaviour of cells.

Nägeli observed that some cells were formed by the division of other cells but he thought that new cells could be formed out of the nucleus alone and believed that both cells and their nuclei could be formed in more than one way.

In 1856, the pathologist Rudolf Virchow (1821–1902) published the results of his microscope work and rejected the idea that cells, or anything else, could arise by spontaneous generation. He argued that all cells were made out of already existing cells, *omnis cellula e cellula*, although he did not know how. Between 1852 and 1862, Robert Remak (1815–1865) showed that cells divided by simple constriction and that all the parts of the cell, the small dark-staining nucleus and the surrounding cytoplasm, were divided up at each cell division so that not only were all cells formed from pre-existing cells but also nuclei appeared to be formed from pre-existing nuclei.

In 1861, the French zoologist Eduard-Girard Balbiani (1825–1899) had the idea of using a weak

Below Cells dividing by constriction. Both cytoplasm and nucleus divides in two. From R. Remak *Müllers Archiv*, 1852.

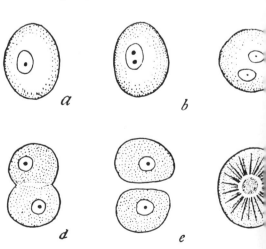

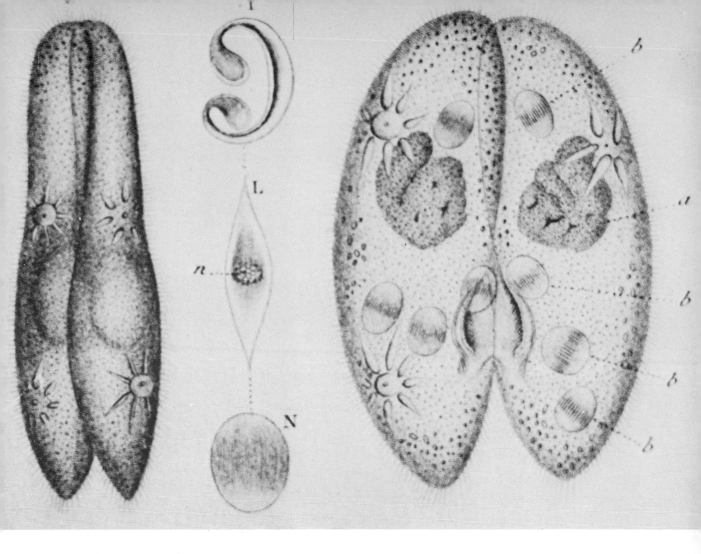

Above Nuclear division in *Paramecium* from E. G. Balbiani 1861. b, dividing nuclei with chromosomes arranged in a band in the middle which Balbiani thought were spermatozoa.

stain so that only parts of the cell stained. Until then, heavy stains had been used to colour the whole object to be viewed under a microscope. Balbiani used a weak solution of carmine dye after fixing in acetic acid.

Balbiani's published pictures of preparations of conjugating single-cell ciliate animals show several stages of nuclear division: small darkly staining blobs arranged on a fibrous spindle. Balbiani thought these blobs were the spermatozoa of *Paramecium*.

Theodor Schwann (1810–1882) co-founder, with Schleiden, of the cell theory had supposed in 1839 that an unfertilized egg could be considered a single

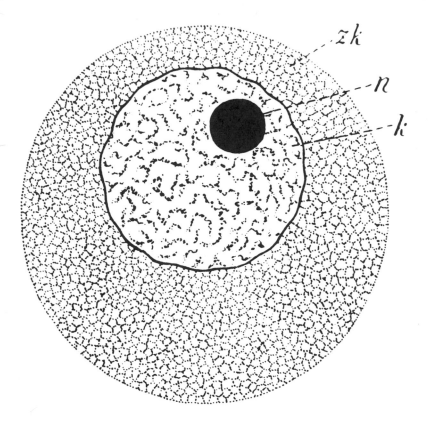

Left Egg cell before fertilization. k is the nucleus, n a dark staining area called the nucleolus. From A. Weismann *Vorträge über Deszendenztheorie*, 1904.

Below Spermatozoa. e is a human spermatozoon (W. George, 1965).

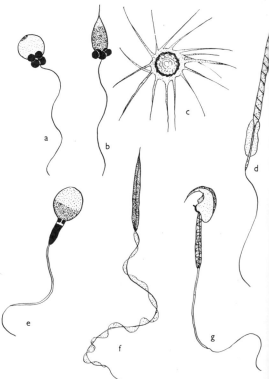

cell with nucleus and cytoplasm and, in 1841, Albert Kölliker (1817–1905) had considered the spermatozoon to be a single nucleus. Then followed the observations of Amici in 1847 and of Pringsheim in 1856 who showed that single cells fuse at fertilization to provide the cell from which the new organism develops.

But it was not until 1876 that it was realized by Oscar Hertwig (1849–1922) that it is the nuclei that are important in fertilization. He saw two nuclei in a fertilized sea urchin egg and he realized that one of the nuclei was from the spermatozoon and the other from the egg cell. No one at this time, however, understood what happened to the nucleus in ordinary cell division and the generally held view was that the nucleus was dissolved away and then reformed in the two new cells after the cell had divided.

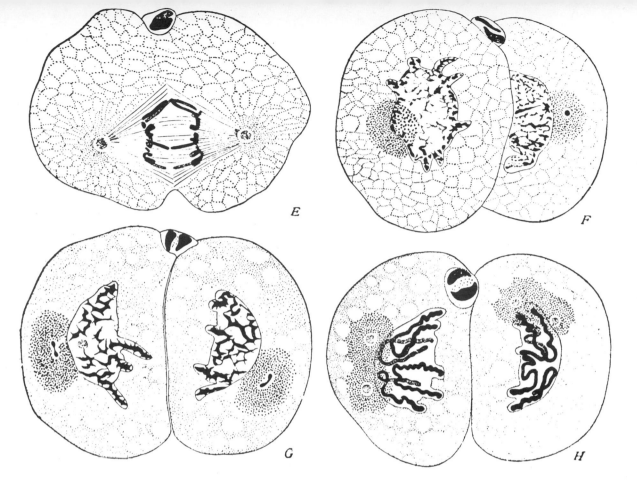

E

F

G

H

Above Mitosis in a developing parasitic roundworm *Ascaris* from T. Boveri *Uber Differenzierung der Zellkerne während der Furchung des Eies von Ascaris,* 1888.

Fifteen years after his original publication, in which nuclear division was clearly figured though not recognized, Balbiani solved the problem.

In 1876, he at last understood the meaning of the dark staining blobs he had seen in *Paramecium.* Working on the cells round the ovary of the grasshopper *Stenobothrus,* Balbiani saw that from the nucleus a number of blobs were formed. These *batonnets,* as he called them, became arranged in a bundle in the centre of the cell, divided in the middle and became two bundles, one of which went into each of the two new cells and formed the new nuclei.

This was the first record of the bodies now known as chromosomes or colour bodies. They were given this name, in 1888, because they stained more heavily than the rest of the nucleus during cell division.

Balbiani was wrong in only one point. He said the *batonnets* divided in half across the middle whereas, in 1879, Walter Flemming (1843–1915) was able to show in salamander cells that the threads divided along their length. It was then quickly realized that this division of the nucleus by mitosis (Flemming's term meaning thread production) occurred in both plants and animals, from the single-cell protozoon to the higher organism.

Based on this recognition of chromosomes dividing equally at cell division, it was soon found that the chromosomes behaved differently during the formation of the eggs and spermatozoa, the egg cells and the pollen grains. Several cytologists (cell-biologists) contributed to the understanding that the number of chromosomes is reduced to half before the eggs and spermatozoa are ready for fertilization. Thus, the number typical of the organism is halved before fertilization and the typical number is again formed in the fertilized zygote from which the new organism grows by a long series of mitotic cell divisions.

In 1905, the division which halved the number of chromosomes in the germ cells became known as meiosis, (reduction).

The advances were made as a result of improving techniques. Different stains were brought in to give more selective pictures than Balbiani had obtained. Sometimes several stains were used to colour different parts of the cell. The advances were made as each man recognized more than the one before. But a man sees only what he is looking for.

Balbiani had made preparations of chromosomes in the dividing nucleus of *Paramecium*. But, because he thought the big nucleus of the protozoon was the ovary and the small one the testis, he saw spermatozoa instead of chromosomes. Many intermediate observations had to be made before Balbiani saw and understood the *batonnets*.

Below Mitosis in two different plants to show the longitudinal splitting of the chromosomes from V. Grégoire *La Cellule*, 1906.

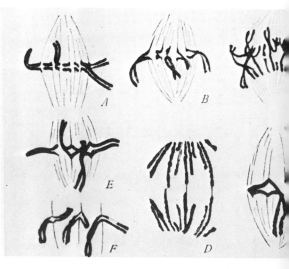

Right August Weismann.

Below Development of a freshwater crustacean to show the ancestral germ cells distinguishable as a separate group, g, from the earliest stages. From E. Korschelt and K. Heider *Lehrbuch der Vergleichenden Entwicklungsgeschichte*, 1902.

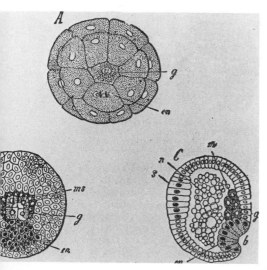

One of the most important figures in the development of biological theory at this time was Weismann.

August Weismann (1834–1914) was Professor of Zoology at the University of Freiburg in Germany. He was able to combine the ideas of inheritance with those of cytologists. Weismann showed that it is the gametes that are important in heredity.

Gametes (germ cells) fuse to form a cell from which a new organism is produced. Early in development, new gamete cells are made by this organism for sending on to the next generation. But the body cells of the organism die.

Weismann seems to have had this idea from studying the growth of flies from eggs. He noticed that, early in development, cells were put aside that would eventually become the cells from which the gametes were made. From this, Weismann concluded that the body cells of the organism do not affect the hereditary capacities of the germ cells.

This made the inheritance of characters acquired during the life of an individual unlikely: cut off the tails of dogs or horses, generation after generation, but they still grow tails.

This was in agreement with what Mendel had found when he grew his different varieties of celandine side by side. They did not become like one another but kept the inherited form of their ancestors. It argued against Darwin's idea of pangenes or gemmules that came from all over the body into the gametes and, in the next generation, determined the form of the organ from which they had come. Pangenes came from the whiskers, for example, to the gametes, were passed on at fertilization and determined and went into the cells of the whiskers of the new organism.

It was in the year of the *batonnets*, ten years after Mendel's paper, that de Vries started work on the hybridization of maize.

In 1889, de Vries published a book called *Intracellular Pangenesis*. His pangene was considered to be a definite material particle and all living organisms were made up of pangenes. De Vries believed that pangenes could be mixed together in any proportions and could explain the results of experiments in hybridization. The seemingly endless variation in the form of the offspring of hybrids could be accounted for by the mixing of the pangenes in various ways.

Three years later, de Vries was investigating crosses between hairy and smooth white campions *Silene*. In the F_2 generation he records the production of 392 hairy plants and 144 smooth. But de Vries deduced nothing from it.

Below Silene alba the white campion from J. Sowerby *English Botany*, 1873.

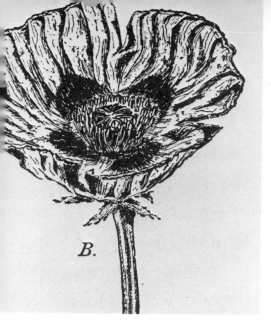

Above A poppy with dark spots at the base of the petals from H. de Vries *The Mutation Theory*, 1910.

He crossed poppies with black marks at the base of the petals with a variety that has white marks at the base. In the second hybrid generation, he had 158 with black marks and 43 with white. The experiments were continued through several generations.

By 1896, de Vries knew about dominance and had discovered the 3 to 1 ratio of the F_2 generation. He also knew that of the three "dominant" types in the F_2 generation only a third bred true and the other two-thirds were, like their parents, hybrid or heterozygous (Bateson's term in 1902 for combined unlike characters). De Vries planned his experiments to show how his pangenes, material particles, were inherited and had come to the same conclusions as Mendel. But he did not publish.

In 1899, when he gave an address to the International Conference of the Royal Horticultural Society, he did not reveal his results. He needed to prove that his theory held true for a great number of plants.

By the end of 1899, de Vries had evidence of the particulate nature of inheritance and segregation from over thirty different species and varieties. He was ready to publish.

Correns understood dominance and the 3 to 1 ratio and that inherited factors could be considered to exist in pairs. He went further and suggested that the pairs of factors segregate sometime during the nuclear divisions that take place in the formation of the pollen grain and egg cell. Correns had the advantage over Mendel of the new cytology with its understanding of cell division.

Tschermak found that tall pea plants seemed to be dominant to short and he obtained a 3 to 1 ratio for yellow and green peas and for smooth and wrinkled.

The Mendelian laws had taken thirty-four years to be discovered by de Vries, Correns and Tschermak. And it was only at this late date that their universality was recognized. None of the three had investigated or formalized the inheritance of more than one character difference at the same time. Mendel's law of independent assortment remained unique.

There was only one more piece to be put into the puzzle before the basic ideas of unit factor inheritance were complete.

In 1902, Correns related the inherited factors to the chromosomes. He supposed the factors to be like beads on a string but he imagined that both factors of a pair were on the same chromosome. Finally, also in 1902, Walter Sutton (1877–1916) of Columbia University in the United States explained the relationship of Mendel's characters, or factors, to the chromosomes.

Working on grasshopper cells, Sutton showed that chromosomes occur in pairs: there are always two that look alike and that are usually distinguishable from all the others. *Brachystola magna,* the grasshopper, has twenty-two chromosomes or eleven pairs of chromosomes. Sutton suggested that this observation might "constitute the physical basis of the Mendelian law of heredity." Pairs of factors were carried on pairs of chromosomes.

Sutton then showed that the pairs of chromosomes come together and then separate one into each gamete during the reduction division of meiosis. This was the physical basis of segregation. So long as the characters were on different chromosomes they would be inherited according to Mendel's law of independent assortment.

This law could not always be true because the characters of an individual "could not exceed the number of chromosomes in the germ products," but as Sutton observed, "it follows that all the allelomorphs [factors] represented by any one chromosome must be inherited together."

Sutton established that many factors could be on the same chromosome and would be inherited together.

Top right The green grasshopper *Brachystola magna* from which Sutton obtained paired chromosomes. From T. de Charpentier *Orthoptera,* 1845.

Centre right Chromosomes of a male grasshopper arranged in pairs (E. E. Carothers, 1913).

Bottom right The beginning of meiosis in the grasshopper *Brachystola* (W. S. Sutton, 1902).

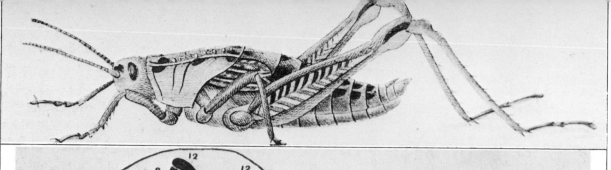

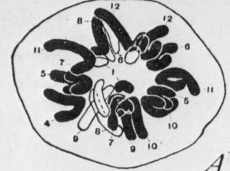

A

B

C

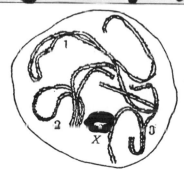

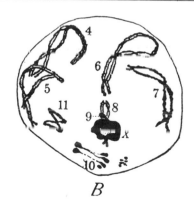

A

B

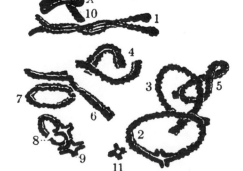

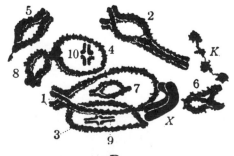

C

D

In 1909 the Dane Wilhelm Johannsen (1857–1927) gave the name gene to Mendel's factors.

If Mendel had never lived and worked in the monastery garden of Brno, the laws of heredity would have been discovered. The de Vriesian laws, as they would have been called, would have made the same impact. The time was right, in 1900, for the laws of heredity to be understood.

Below Commemorative medal to mark the centenary of Mendel's papers on heredity.

Date Chart

1859   *On the Origin of Species by Means of Natural Selection* by C. Darwin.

1863   Mendel's experiments on *Pisum* completed.

1865   8th February and 8th March Mendel reads his papers *Experiments in Plant Hybridization* to the Brno Natural History Society.

Hybridization in the Plant Kingdom by M. Wichura.

1866   *Experiments in Plant Hybridization* by G. Mendel.

1868   Mendel elected Abbot of the monastery.

1869   *Hereditary Genius* by F. Galton.

1881   *Plant Hybrids* by W. O. Focke.

1884   Death of Mendel.

1887   Reduction division of the chromosomes observed by T. Boveri.

1888   First use of the term chromosome.

1889   *Intracellular Pangenesis* by H. de Vries.

1893   *The Germ-plasm: a Theory of Heredity* by A. Weismann.

1900   April: *On the Law of Segregation in Hybrids* by H. de Vries.

May: *G. Mendel's Law of the Behaviour of the Progeny of Hybrid Races* by C. Correns.

June: *On Experimental Crosses in Pisum sativum* by E. von Tschermak.

1902   *Mendel's Principles of Heredity* by W. Bateson.

1903   *On the Morphology of the Chromosome Group in Brachystola magna* by W. S. Sutton.

1909   *Elements of Heredity* by W. Johannsen.

Glossary

ALGA (*alga*, seaweed)   Plant without roots, stems or leaves which makes its own food by photosynthesis and is usually aquatic.

ALLELOMORPH (ALLELE) (*allelone*, in turn; *morphe*, form)   One of a pair of hereditary factors or genes.

APOMIXIS (*apo*, away; *mixis*, mingling)   Reproduction without the fusion of germ cells.

ASCARIS (*askaris*, intestinal worm)   A round worm parasitic in the gut of man and other mammals.

BACK CROSS   A cross between an offspring and one of the parent types.

BLOOD GROUPS   Groups of people or animals whose blood can be mixed without clotting. The best known are the A, B, O series. The red blood cells may carry proteins A or B or both (AB) on their surfaces or no protein (O). Each protein depends on a gene inherited in the normal Mendelian way. Blood group AB people have genes for both proteins and both are found on their red blood cells. Group O are genetically OO and carry no protein. Group A may be genetically AA or OA but in either case has protein A on its blood cells. Similarly, group B may be BB or OB with protein B on the cells.

BOTYS MARGARITALIS   Pearl moth.

BRACHYSTOLA MAGNA   An American long horned green grasshopper.

BRASSICA RAPA   Turnip.

BRUCHUS PISI   The pea-weevil.

CELL (*cella*, storeroom)   The unit of structure and function of plants and animals. Made up of a complex of membranes and usually containing a nucleus. The outside is clearly limited by a membrane or cell wall.

CELL THEORY   The theory that all plants and animals are made up of cells.

CHROMOSOME (*chroma*, colour; *soma*, body)   Dark staining threads in the nucleus of all cells, each thread made up of many units of heredity. Number usually constant for each species.

CYTOLOGY (*kytos*, cell; *logos*, discourse)   The study of cells.

CYTOPLASM (*kytos*, cell; *plasma*, form)   The substance of the cell, excluding the nucleus, composed of a complex of membranes.

DIANTHUS   Pinks, carnations.

ARENARIUS   Sand pink.

CARYOPHYLLUS   Clove pink.

CHINENSIS   Chinese pink.

PLUMARIUS   Feathery pink.

SUPERBUS   Superb white pink.

DIGITALIS PURPUREA   Foxglove.

DOMINANT CHARACTER (*dominus*, ruler)   Inherited unit that appears to mask its partner in a hybrid.

EMBRYO (*embryon*, foetus)   A developing plant or animal.

EMBRYO SAC   The part of the ovary that contains the egg cell and several nuclei which are concerned with providing food for the developing plant.

F_1 First filial generation. The first generation of offspring from any cross.

F_2 Second filial generation. The generation produced by crossing individuals of the F_1 generation.

F_3 Third filial generation. The generation produced by crossing individuals of the F_2 generation.

FERTILIZATION   (*fero*, to bear)   The fusion of male and female germ cells.

FLORET (*flos*, flower)   One of a cluster of small flowers that go to make a flower head as in hawkweeds and dandelions.

FUSE (*fundere*, melt, blend)   Of germ cells when male and female cells come together to form one new cell.

GAMETE (*gamete(s)*, wife or husband)   The germ cells that unite to form a new cell from which the offspring develops.

GEMMULE (*gemma*, a bud)   Particles once thought to be made in all parts of the body and sent to the germ cells for passing on to the next generation.

GENE (*genesis*, origin, descent)   The unit of heredity forming part of a chromosome and determining the way in which characters are formed in the developing plant or animal.

GENETICS   The science of genes and heredity.

GENOTYPE (*genesis*, origin, descent; *typos*, image, type) All the genes of a particular plant or animal.

GERM CELL (*germen,* bud) The cells that unite to form a new cell from which the offspring develops.

GEUM URBANUM Herb Bennet or wood avens.

HETEROZYGOUS (*heteros*, other; *zygos*, yoke) Having paired unlike genes.

HIERACIUM PILOSELLA Mouse-ear hawkweed or creeping hawkweed.

HOMOZYGOUS (*homos*, alike; *zygos*, yoke) Having paired like genes.

HYBRID (*hybrida*, mongrel) The offspring of unlike parents.

HYBRIDIZATION Making hybrids by crossing unlike parents.

KEEL The two lower petals of flowers of the pea family which form an envelope round the reproductive parts of the flower.

MEIOSIS (*meiosis*, reduction) A division of the nucleus in which the number of chromosomes, and hereditary units, is halved.

MIRABILIS JALAPA Marvel of Peru or four o'clock.

MITOSIS (*mitos*, thread) A division of the nucleus which results in two identical new nuclei with the same number of chromosomes as the original.

MOINA A crustacean water flea.

NICOTIANA Tobacco plants.

PANICULATA Panicled tobacco plant.

RUSTICANA "Turkish" tobacco plant.

NUCLEUS (*nucleus*, kernel, inner part) The part of the cell that contains the chromosomes.

OEDOGONIUM A freshwater filamentous green alga

ORGANISM (*organon*, organ; *ismos*, condition) A living thing.

OVARY (*ovarium*, ovary) The part of the plant or animal that contains the female germ cells.

P₁ First parental generation. The individuals from which the first cross is made.

PANGENE (*pan*, all; *genesis*, origin, descent) Used in the same way as gemmule: particles once thought to be made in all parts of the body and sent to the germ cells for passing on to the next generation. Used by de Vries to mean almost the same thing as the modern gene: a unit of heredity.

PARAMECIUM   The slipper animalcule. A single celled freshwater animal covered in cilia.

PATHOLOGY (*pathos*, suffering; *logos*, discourse)   The study of diseases.

PHANEROGAM (*phaneros*, visible; *gamos*, marriage)   Any plant that makes seeds.

PHASEOLUS   Runner beans.

PHENOTYPE (*phaneros*, visible; *typos*, image, type)   The appearance of a plant or animal resulting from the interaction of its genes and its surroundings.

PISUM SATIVUM   Edible pea.

POLLEN (*pollen*, fine flour)   The male germ cells of flowering plants.

POLLEN GRAIN   A single male germ cell of a flowering plant.

POLLEN TUBE   An outpushing from a pollen grain that grows down the style to the ovary of a flowering plant.

PROTEIN   One of the three main chemical compounds that make up living matter (the others are fats and carbohydrates). Hair, muscle and red blood pigment, for example, are proteins.

PROTOZOON (*protos*, first; *zoon*, animal)   Single celled animal.

PURE LINE   A line obtained by mating only like individuals for many generations.

RANUNCULUS FICARIA   Lesser celandine.

RECESSIVE CHARACTER (*recedere*, to retire)   Inherited unit that does not show when paired with a dominant but only when paired with another like itself.

RECIPROCAL CROSS (*reciprocus*, having a backward and forward motion)   A cross made between two varieties in which each, in turn, provides the male parent.

REDUCTION DIVISION (*reducere,* to bring back or down)   Meiosis. A division of the nucleus in which the number of chromosomes, and hereditary units, is halved.

SALIX   Willows.

PURPUREA   Bitter purple willow.

VIMINALIS   Osier.

SILENE ALBA   White campion.

SPECIES (*species*, sort) A group of similar and interbreeding plants or animals.

SPERMATOZOON (*sperma*, seed; *zoon*, animal) The male germ cell.

STAMEN (*stamen*, thread) The male, pollen producing, organs of a flowering plant. Made up of a fine stalk and a pollen sac.

STENOBOTHRUS The stripe-winged grasshopper.

STIGMA (*stigma*, point) Expanded tip of the style for receiving pollen in flowering plants.

STYLE (*stylos*, pillar) Column of tissue arising from the ovary and down which the pollen tube grows in a flowering plant.

TESTIS (*testes*, testicle) The part of an animal that contains the male germ cells.

TRAGOPOGON Goat's-beard or salsify.

VARIETY (*vario*, to change) Plants or animals that differ from other members of their species.

VERONICA Speedwells.

ZYGOTE (*zygos*, yoke) The cell formed from the fusion of male and female germ cells from which the embryo develops.

Further Reading

Dunn, L. C. (ed.) *Genetics in the Twentieth Century* (Macmillan, New York, 1951)

George, W. *Elementary Genetics* (Macmillan 1965)

Hughes, A. *A History of Cytology* (Abelard-Schuman 1959)

Iltis, H. *Life of Mendel* (George Allen & Unwin 1932)

Mendel, G. *Experiments in Plant Hybridisation* edited by J. H. Bennett (Oliver & Boyd 1965)

Olby, R. *Origins of Mendelism* (Constable 1966)

Peters, J. A. *Classic Papers in Genetics* (Prentice-Hall 1959)

Roberts, H. F. *Plant Hybridization before Mendel* (Hafner 1929)

Sturtevant, A. H. *A History of Genetics* (Harper Row 1965)

Index

Acknowledgements

The author and publisher thank all those who have given their kind permission for reproduction of the illustrations that appear on the following pages:
British Library Board, 12, 35, 73 top; Curators of the Bodleian Library, 8 bottom, 26; Librarian of the Botany School, Oxford University, 30, 31, 33, 38, 41, 63 bottom, 66; Librarian of Lady Margaret Hall, Oxford, 36, 37, 43, 58, 63 top, 73 bottom, 82; Macmillan Press Limited, 78 bottom; Dr. Vitezlav Orel of the Moravian Museum, Brno, *frontispiece,* 10, 14, 15, 16, 17, 18, 19, 20, 21, 22, 23, 27 top, 28 top, 46, 48, 50, 57, 59, 61, 62, 64, 65, 67, 68, 69; Science Museum, 8 top; Dr. George Varley of the Hope Department, Oxford University, 27 bottom, 85 top.

The author also wishes to thank George Crowther for his criticism and Gareth Stevens for his constructive editing.